RADICALS

RADICALS

PORTRAITS OF A DESTRUCTIVE PASSION

DAVID HOROWITZ

Since 1947
REGNERY
PUBLISHING, INC.
An Eagle Publishing Company • Washington, DC

Cataloging-in-Publication data on file with the Library of Congress
ISBN 978-1-59698-812-5

Published in the United States by
Regnery Publishing, Inc.
One Massachusetts Avenue NW
Washington, DC 20001
www.Regnery.com

Manufactured in the United States of America
10 9 8 7 6 5 4 3 2 1

Books are available in quantity for promotional or premium use. Write to Director of Special Sales, Regnery Publishing, Inc., One Massachusetts Avenue NW, Washington, DC 20001, for information on discounts and terms, or call (202) 216-0600.

Distributed to the trade by
Perseus Distribution
250 West 57th Street
New York, NY 10107

*But I, with my memory—all the dead and the mad
are in my custody, and I am
the nemesis of the would-be forgotten.*
—**Saul Bellow,** *Herzog*

Contents

INTRODUCTION

A Universal Aspiration

1

CHAPTER ONE

The Two Christophers

7

CHAPTER TWO

Feminist Accuser

57

CHAPTER THREE

Cultural Decline

99

CHAPTER FOUR

Pardoned Bombers

127

CHAPTER FIVE

Liberated Woman

155

CHAPTER SIX

A Radical Machiavelli

171

Notes

199

Index

219

A Universal Aspiration

All the totalitarian movements of modernity have been inspired by the same fantasy of a world made right and finally brought into harmony with itself. This utopian delusion is not restricted to aspiring commissars or religious fanatics. In one form or another, it is the ideal of every believer in a universal progress, including those who would be dismayed to think of themselves in such destructive company.

The desire to make things better is an impulse essential to our humanity. But taken beyond the limits of what is humanly possible, the same hope is transformed into a destructive passion, until it becomes a desire to annihilate whatever stands in the way of the beautiful idea. Nihilism is thus the practical extreme of the radical project. Consequently, the fantasy of a redeemed future has repeatedly led to catastrophic results as progressive radicals pursue their impossible schemes. It is an enduring irony of the human condition that the urgency to make the world "a better place" is also the chief source of the suffering that human beings have inflicted on each other from the beginning of time.

The present volume focuses on individuals who are adherents of the progressive faith, a label that has been embraced by Marxists and anarchists, socialists and liberals alike. "Radical" normally connotes a sharp and violent break with the existing order, which would suggest that the careers described in these pages were confined to the fringes of the political culture. Nothing could be further from the truth. Christopher Hitchens was an internationally celebrated journalist and author; Bettina Aptheker is an acclaimed professor at an elite university; and Cornel West is a celebrity academic who has been friends with two Democratic presidents, and is the author of bestselling books praised by arbiters of the literary culture. Saul Alinsky, a prominent figure in the radical Sixties posthumously became the political guide to an entire generation of American progressives, including an occupant of the Oval Office.

Radicals have often been described as "liberals in a hurry"—sharing similar goals but with expectations that were high and timetables that were short. These are indeed attributes of the terrorists Kathy Boudin and Susan Rosenberg, whose stories are told in this text. But far from being condemned by liberals who would not themselves think of committing their crimes, they have been treated as spiritual comrades, and embraced as victims of a society whose injustices encouraged them to commit their desperate acts. Liberals of this disposition were once referred to as "fellow travelers," people who failed to muster the courage of their convictions but nonetheless shared the radical dream of a universal progress and a world that would be socially just.

The type of this fellow traveler was dissected in a famous Cold War novel by Lionel Trilling in the character of John Laksell.[1] Men like Laksell, Trilling observed, were not actually *for* communism, but were convinced that "one was morally compromised, turned toward evil and away from good, if one was against it." Because Laksell did not oppose the Communists' vision of a liberated future, he was unable to oppose the war that Communists had declared on the society they actually inhabited. Laksell refused to become an anti-Communist and join the war against totalitarianism, Trilling explained, because "one could not oppose [Communist ideas] without being illiberal, even reactionary. One would have to have something better to offer and Laksell had nothing better. He could not even imagine what the better ideas would be."[2] Laksell therefore became an "anti-anti-Communist," and took his stand as an opponent of those who opposed the Marxist totalitarian idea.

Sixty years later, Trilling's observations apply to the fellow travelers of radicalism, who are generally referred to as liberals, and who make up the expansive ranks of the progressive cause. They refuse to oppose the fundamental ideas behind the radicals' assault on free societies because to do so would make them illiberal and reactionary and put them in the camp of the conservative right. The failure of these fellow travelers to oppose radical ideas explains the success radicals have achieved in pushing their cause beyond the social margins. Over the last several decades, the radical critique of American democracy has become the curriculum of American universities, and the culture of its liberal elites—a fact reflected in the otherwise inexplicable career of Professor Cornel West, which is described in the pages that follow.[3]

Once a partisan of the progressive cause, I have devoted myself since leaving its ranks to an effort to comprehend it—first to understand what prompts people to believe in world-encompassing and world-transforming myths; and second, to explore the tragic consequences of the attempts to act on them. This was the subject of *Radical Son*, an autobiography published in 1997, and of a series of essays and books I have written over the last twenty years, including *Destructive Generation*, *The Politics of Bad Faith*, *Unholy Alliance*, and *Left Illusions*. I have also written two small volumes, *The End of Time* and *A Point in Time*, which explore the way the radical passion is a religious response to our common human fate. The present work is perhaps the last I will write about a subject that has occupied me in one way or another over the course of a lifetime.

When all is said and done, what has impressed me most, after all these years, is how little we human beings are able to learn collectively from our experience, how slowly we do learn, and how quickly we forget.

———

The chapters that follow begin with an inquiry into the life and thought of Christopher Hitchens, a writer who had serious second thoughts about some of his radical commitments but was unable to leave the progressive faith. Hitchens' life and work offer an opportunity to examine the issues that define a radical outlook, and the moral and intellectual incoherence that overtake an intelligent mind whose second thoughts remain incomplete.

The second chapter follows the life of an icon of radical feminism, and is a study in the totalitarian quest for a unity of the political and the personal. We are all prisoners of what Hegel called an "unhappy consciousness," reflecting the division between the world and the self. Radicals seek to overcome this division by creating a new world that will resolve this dilemma. The practical result of this effort is the embrace of a totalitarian politics and the inevitable detachment of the individual from her own reality.

The third chapter follows the improbable career of Professor Cornel West, a remarkably shallow intellect whose rise to cultural eminence has been made possible by his personification of progressive clichés. His career is consequently a reflection of a general cultural decline.

The fourth chapter focuses on a group of individuals who are best described as "Nechaevists," after the nineteenth-century Russian terrorist of that name—privileged youth who jettison the opportunities bestowed on them by a generous society to become criminals in the service of a political idea. It is also a tale of the Laksells, perched comfortably on the heights of society and culture, who work assiduously to create sympathy for the perpetrators of indefensible deeds.

The fifth chapter diverges from the others as the story of an unpolitical woman whose coming of age in a political decade encouraged her to pursue the idea of self-liberation to the point of personal disaster. Following decades of drug abuse and descent into chaos, she finally rescued herself from ruin by rejecting her identity as a cultural victim to grasp the specific truth of her life.

A final chapter examines the prescriptive advice of Saul Alinsky, mentor to the present generation of post-Communist progressives. It explores the paradox at the heart of the utopian outlook—that its idealism is a nihilism—providing a summary statement of the central theme of this book.

Earlier versions of these chapters have appeared as articles in FrontPageMag.com and NationalReviewOnline.com. They have been edited for this volume and in several instances re-written.

CHAPTER ONE

The Two Christophers

(Or the Importance of Second Thoughts)

I first met Christopher Hitchens in 1970 when I was editing *Ramparts* magazine, which was then the largest publication of the left. Christopher was ten years my junior and fresh out of Oxford, embarking on his first adventure in the New World. When he stopped in at my Berkeley office looking for guidance, one of the questions he asked me in all seriousness was, "Where is the working class?" Only the devout left—the "holy rollers" as I by that time regarded them—could still think this mythical entity was an actual force in a nation where classes were social relics, and every man was king. But rather than make this an issue, I directed my visitor to the local Trotskyists, who were true believers, failing to realize that he was one of them.

Our next encounter took place a dozen years later, also in Berkeley, and was not nearly as pleasant. By then I had rejected most tenets of the radical faith, although I had not publicly left its ranks. We met at a small lunch attended by several *Nation* editors, among them Victor Navasky and Kai Bird. Before long the conversation turned to the Middle East and the war in Lebanon, and I found myself confronting what in those days we referred to as a political "gut check." What was my attitude, Christopher wanted to know, towards Israel's invasion of Lebanon? The goal of the Israeli offensive was to clear out PLO terrorists who had entrenched themselves behind an international border in southern Lebanon and were shelling towns in northern Israel. The left's attitude was that Israel was an imperialist pawn of the United States and oppressor of Palestinians. Leftists were therefore opposed to Israel's effort to protect itself. My second thoughts had led me to the conclusion that I was not, and I rose imprudently to Christopher's provocation: "This is the first Israeli war I have supported," I said, which ended any fraternal possibilities for the remaining conversation.

Two years later, my co-author Peter Collier and I voted for Ronald Reagan, and three years after that we organized a "Second Thoughts" conference, bringing together other former radicals who had become supporters of the anti-Communist cause. Christopher came to our conference with his *Nation* cohort Alex Cockburn to attack us. In the column he filed after our event, he described our suggestion that second thoughts might be superior to first ones as "smug," and singled out my remark that supporting America's enemies should be considered treason as "sinister."[1] He subsequently elaborated his feelings about those who had abandoned the leftist cause in a brutal article about the writer Paul Johnson, sneering at his "well advertised stagger from left to right," which Christopher regarded as the venal maneuver of someone "who, having lost his faith, believes that he had found his reason."[2] (And why not?)

But times change, and subsequently Christopher himself became associated by others—not entirely correctly—with a generation of post-9/11 second-thoughters. Revising some of his attitudes towards the left and its loyalties, he had vaunted a patriotism towards America he would once have thought of as, well, sinister. A climactic moment in this odyssey—or so it should have been—was the publication of an engrossing memoir of a life, heretical at both ends, which he called *Hitch-22*. Among its other virtues, the book provided a fertile occasion for those of us who preceded him to take another look at our own second thoughts, and measure the distances that we, and our one-time antagonist, had traveled.

The man his friends called "Hitch" was a figure of such unruly contradictions it may be said of him, as Dr. Johnson said of the metaphysical poets, that he had "the ability to yoke heterogeneous ideas by violence together." Opponent of America's war in Vietnam and supporter of America's war in Iraq; libertarian defender of free market capitalism and impenitent admirer of Trotsky and Marx; pro-lifer and feminist doctrinaire; friend to both Paul Wolfowitz, neo-conservative hawk, and to Victor Navasky, apologist for Alger Hiss, the Rosenbergs, and Hamas.

Christopher eagerly embraced not only incompatible ideas and unlikely comrades but divergent modes of being: both a political renegade and keeper of the flame; fierce partisan and practiced ironist; post-modern skeptic and romantic nostalgist; one-dimensional polemicist and literary polymath; passionate moralist and calculating operator; hard-headed critic and dewy-eyed sentimentalist; serious thinker and determined attention grabber; irreverent contrarian and serenader of the choir; self-styled Man of the People and accomplished social climber; and—most inexplicable of all—Oxonian gentleman and master of vitriol.

Among the things to be discovered reading Christopher's memoir is that there are not many things you will figure out about him that he had not already thought of himself. His chronicle opens with a superbly realized account of personal origins, containing portraits of his conservative Anglican father and his rebellious, romantic, and secretly Jewish mother, "two much opposed and sharply discrepant ancestral stems: two stray branches that only war and chance could ever have caused to become entwined."[3] On the one side the mother, Yvonne, an alien who refused to know her place; on the other, the father, a naval officer referred to by the son as "the Commander," who knew his place and served his country. "Sending a Nazi convoy raider to the bottom," his radical offspring observes in a typically inscrutable Hitchens tribute, "is a better day's work than any I have ever done."[4]

Those familiar with Hitchens' writing have long appreciated his stylistic elegance. But it was not until the publication of his memoir that he showed he was also a wily operator, for whom Homer's epithet for Ulysses—"deep devising"—is particularly apt, using his roguish charm and sparkling literacy to eat his cake and have it too, stutter-stepping past potentially inconvenient truths.

At the outset, the reader is alerted to Christopher's conscious pursuit of "the Janus-faced mode of life."[5] The figure Janus was the Roman god of temple doorways, who looks both ways and is invariably depicted in his statuary with two faces. Grabbing the horns of his own enigma, Christopher observes that the doors of the temple were open in time of war, and that war "is a time when the ideas of contradiction and conflict are most naturally regnant." The most intense wars, he also notes, are civil, and the most rending conflicts internal. "What I hope to do now," he says of the text to come, "is give some idea of what it is like to fight on two fronts at once, to try and keep opposing ideas alive in the same mind, even occasionally to show two faces at the same time."[6]

It is the initial salvo in a campaign to defend a life that aspired to moral authenticity but often seemed to skirt the edge of having it both ways, a tendency that provided his most determined enemies with an irresistible target. In the *New Statesman*, the Marxist literary critic Terry Eagleton castigated him thus: "It is as though he sees his own double-dealing as a rather agreeable versatility—as testimony to his myriad-mindedness rather than as a privileged, spoilt-brat desire (among other things) to hog it all."[7] Characteristically, Hitchens does not duck his contradictions in this memoir but embraces them, making no effort to hide the determination to keep "double-entry books." Describing an occasion on which his radical comrades caught him fraternizing with John Sparrow, a notorious symbol of the reactionary ruling caste at Oxford, Christopher writes: "I could have taken refuge in some 'know your enemy' formulation but something in me said that this would be ignoble. I didn't want a one-dimensional politicized life."[8]

Whatever may be said of these choices, they are an undeniable source of Christopher's appeal as an *enfant terrible*, the reason he is far more interesting than Eagleton or any of his leftwing critics with whom, this memoir shows, he still shared fundamental beliefs. It is why reading his book—regardless of whether one agrees with the politics or finds them repellent or merely confusing—is an enterprise that is rewarding and often a delight. But Christopher's express desire not to be confined to a single standard does not explain the life that unfolded along multiple paths, nor does it put to rest the ethical questions that continue to dog them.

In attempting to understand Christopher's politics and to understand *him*, the reader of his book is continually frustrated by a troubling lacuna at the heart of the text—a Hitch-22 as it were. Inexplicably for a writer so keenly observant of the world around him, Christopher's attempt at a self-portrait lacks the introspective curiosity integral to such a task or the interior probing that would unwrap his mysteries both for himself and others.

A dozen years before Christopher's book appeared, I was at a similar age and also wrote a memoir. One of my purposes was to give an account of the path I had traveled away from the Marxist views and socialist crusade that had previously shaped my life. Here is the way I described the point at which I finally came to reject these beliefs: "In that very moment a previously unthinkable possibility… entered my head: The Marxist idea, to which I had devoted my entire intellectual life and work was false…. For the first time in my conscious life I was looking at myself in my human nakedness, without the support of revolutionary hopes, without the faith in a revolutionary future—without the sense of self-importance conferred by the role I would play in remaking the world. For the first time in my life I confronted myself as I really was in the endless march of human coming and going. *I was nothing*."[9]

The crisis that followed this realization became a crucible of despair from which I was able to free myself only when I was able to replace the myths that had sustained me with other reasons to go on. But in Christopher's account of his life, there is no such moment of crisis and no such self-encounter, despite the fact that the journey he describes would seem to have warranted both. The conclusion to be drawn from this void is that through all his surface changes, Christopher never felt a real subtraction from himself. At every stage of his career he was in his own eyes exactly what he had always been except more so. Each twist in the road presented an opportunity for the accretion of complexity, making an ever more intriguing spectacle for his observers. As my colleague Peter Collier put it, "Christopher was an oyster always working on his own pearl."

Even if there was no such dark night of the soul when Christopher decided to abandon his hostility to a nation he had long been at war with and to defend a symbol of the system he despised, such a night certainly took place much earlier, when as a young man fresh out of college he was climbing onto the wave of the revolutionary future. The life-changing event was the suicide of his mother, Yvonne, then still a young woman. She killed herself in a hotel room in Athens after making a pact with the clergyman she had run off with and taken as a lover. It was, Christopher concedes, a "lacerating, howling moment in my life."[10] He was all of twenty-four.

But in Christopher's memoir there is no elaboration of how this trauma may have affected him, no indication of how so searing a loss and maternal betrayal may have impacted the double lives he pursued, the personal and political triangles he indulged, and the fracturing of commitments to comrades and friends that followed. It is left for the reader to speculate about these matters from a text that denies the very elements that are essential to the task.

Although Christopher was married twice and had other romantic attachments including a briefly mentioned affair with the sister of novelist Martin Amis, none really appear in the 400-page book he wrote about himself. Of Christopher's first wife, a Greek Cypriot lawyer and the mother of his two oldest children, we are told nothing, not even her name. Carol, his second wife, is mentioned several times in passing, but we are never introduced to her and there are no descriptions to put flesh on the woman he shared the last decades of his life with, no attempt to convey how he actually felt toward her or for that matter toward marriage itself. Of his children he writes mainly to concede his guilt over his absence as a father.

But when it comes to Yvonne, whose chapter-length portrait opens the book, the texture is quite different and his feelings rise rapidly to the surface: "Yvonne then was the exotic and the sunlit when I could easily have had a boyhood of stern and dutiful English gray. She was the cream in the coffee, the gin in the Campari, the offer of wine or champagne instead of beer, the laugh in the face of bores and purse-mouths and skinflints, the insurance against bigots and prudes." In a single sentence that closes his account of her life and death, he provides a glimpse of their influence on his own: "Her defeat and despair were also mine for a long time, but I have reason to know that she wanted me to withstand the woe, and when I once heard myself telling someone that she had allowed me a 'second identity,' I quickly checked myself and thought no, perhaps with luck she had represented my first and truest one."[11]

His truest identity. At this point on the page a reader expects the author's gaze to continue inward exploring the vein just opened. Instead, the text abruptly interrupts itself and presents the reader with a set piece under this cold heading: "A *Coda* on the Question of Self-Slaughter"—as though the author were writing about anyone but his mother. In the ensuing passage, the reflections are abstract and the tone that of an academic paper on the psychology and sociology of suicide as perceived in the writings of Emile Durkheim, A.A. Alvarez, and Sylvia Plath. The author tells the reader that this research reflects a quest he has pursued over "four decades," revealing without actually conceding it, that the pain in fact did not go away. But why then engage in this pedantic distraction from the turmoil in his heart which tells us nothing about the trauma to his soul? Partly because he is the enemy of moist sentiments; but also because this gratuitous erudition is a squid's ink to cover his decision not to use the hair pin his mother offers him, in her life and in her death, to pick his own lock. As a memoirist, Hitchens was as *sui generis* as he was in other avenues of his life—not really wishing to be known by others or by himself.[12]

In his portrait of Yvonne, the son describes his mother as the power behind his future throne. "If there is going to be an upper class in this country," she vows, "Christopher is going to be in it."[13] Despite the constraints of their circumstances, Yvonne sent Christopher to infiltrate England's Protestant establishment, first at a posh private school the family could barely afford, and then to Balliol College Oxford to join the upper crust. Yvonne was in her own person a secret agent, a displaced Polish Jew who in marrying the Commander had infiltrated an alien, anti-Semitic culture, hiding her true identity from those closest to her in order to provide herself and her children opportunities they would otherwise have been denied.

How did this matrilineal romance and its tragic ending affect Christopher's attitude toward the sunny tomorrows his comrades pursued? How did it color his optimism about the quest for social justice? (Where, he might have asked, was the justice for *him*? For *Yvonne*?) Christopher is silent. Of the anarchistic upheavals in France in 1968, he writes: "If you have never yourself had the experience of feeling that you are hooked to the great steam engine of history, then allow me to inform you that the conviction is a very intoxicating one."[14] What is the need of the individual soul for this intoxication? What was *Christopher's* need? What happens when the engine and the feelings stop? Christopher makes no attempt to provide answers, nor does it seem likely that he even asked himself the questions.

All the while he was making his way through private schools and burrowing into the inner sanctums of the establishment, Christopher was simultaneously becoming a social rebel, taking the very skills those venerable institutions placed in his hands and putting them into the service of the war a radical generation was waging against them. Yet, even his commitment to rebellion was only half-made, or not so much made as hedged: "I was slowly being inducted into a revolution within the revolution, or to a Left that was in and yet not of the 'Left' as it was generally understood. This perfectly suited my already-acquired and protective habit of keeping two sets of books."[15] Or of being a secret agent in a world he never allowed himself to fully assimilate to.

The leftist sect Christopher joined was actually more convoluted and insulated from normal accountabilities than his narrative suggests. It was a revolution *within* "the revolution *within* the revolution." Trotskyism could be said to be a revolution within the revolution. But the International Socialists, whom Christopher joined, were a Trotskyist splinter consisting of a hundred or so members who were opposed not only to Stalinism but to the Trotskyist mainstream. They separated themselves from other Trotskyists (and from Trotsky himself) who attacked Stalinism but still defended the Soviet Union. Trotskyists who followed "the Old Man" regarded themselves as "Bolsheviks" and viewed Russia as a "deformed" socialist state. By contrast, Hitchens' sect regarded the Soviet Union as having reverted to capitalism and therefore as having joined the enemy. This allowed the group to continue their attacks on the democracies of the West without having to defend "actually existing" socialism in Russia and make excuses for the totalitarian state their fellow Marxists had created.

How does Hitchens view this scholastically precious politics of his youth, or interpret its significance in his memoir? Typically, he doesn't say. But there is another witness, a Hitchens foil so to speak, who provides a telling insight into this puzzle. Peter Hitchens is Christopher's younger brother by two years but, like Christopher's wives, is virtually invisible in Christopher's text, despite the fact that they followed similar political paths. Peter joined the same International Socialist sect in the same era and later came to have second thoughts. But unlike Christopher, Peter eventually became a religious conservative with no ambivalent attitudes towards his previous leftist commitments.

Peter's commentary on Christopher's Trotskyist sect is this: "The [mainstream Trotskyists] were more honest than we were. Ours was the extreme version of pretending that the USSR was not the fault of socialists, or even of Bolsheviks (which we wished to be). Of course it was their fault, the fault of people exactly like us, but we closed our minds to this with a web of excuses. We pretended not to be who we were, and that the USSR was not what it was."[16]

Christopher does not acknowledge that he pretended not to be who he was, and expresses no such second thoughts. On the contrary, his text is rich in late attitudes that are strikingly consistent with the views he held as a youth. "Where it was easy to do so," brother Peter writes of the International Socialists, "we supported causes—the National Liberation Front in Vietnam in particular—whose objects were to extend Soviet power."[17] The fact that the Vietnamese Communists, whom the New Left idolized, were minions of the totalitarian empire that Stalin had built was one of the realizations that turned Peter Collier and myself to second thoughts. When America quit the field of battle in Vietnam under pressure from the anti-war left, and the Communists proceeded to slaughter millions of innocents without protest from that left, we recoiled in horror at what our campaigns had made possible, and what those commitments proved to be, and we said goodbye to all that.

Not so Christopher, who remains loyal in his memoir to the "anti-war" positions he held at the time, regarding the Communists as liberators and the Americans who opposed them as oppressor villains: "The United States was conducting an imperialist war in Indo-China, and a holding action against the insistent demands of its own long-oppressed black minority at home."[18] These are troublingly deceitful remarks. What holding action would Christopher be referring to? The American civil rights movement was supported by the entire nation outside the Deep South, including the White Houses of both Kennedy and the southerner Lyndon Johnson. What America was resisting the insistent demands of the black minority at home? And what imperialist war could he be thinking of? The one bruited in a famous malapropism of Jane Fonda, who claimed that America was in Vietnam for the "tung and the tinsten"? Or is Christopher ventriloquizing Ho Chi Minh Speak and claiming that Americans wanted to replace the French as colonial masters of Indo-China?

Writing of his own participation in a "vast demonstration" against the war, which took place in front of the American Embassy in London, Christopher recalls "the way in which my throat and heart seemed to swell as the police were temporarily driven back and the advancing allies of the Vietnamese began to sing 'We Shall Overcome.'" He then pats himself on the back: "I added to my police record for arrests, of all of which I am still reasonably proud."[19] But why would he be proud of his arrest in a demonstration supporting the Communist conquerors of Cambodia and South Vietnam? Christopher's anti-war comrades, the International Socialists among them, were not "allies of the Vietnamese," as Christopher writes, but allies of the Vietnamese *Communists*, as brother Peter points out, and therefore of the Soviet empire behind them. What these leftists and their Communist heroes actually achieved in Indo-China was one of the worst genocides in history and a long totalitarian night for the Cambodians and the Vietnamese.

To have remained an unreconstructed New Leftist into the twenty-first century was a particularly problematic failing for a man whose model was George Orwell and whose political persona was consciously framed by a perceived moral authority. In a statement that amounts to a one-sentence credo, Christopher writes in his memoir: "The synthesis for which one aimed was the Orwellian one of evolving a consistent and integral anti-totalitarianism."[20] But apparently not for the Cambodians and Vietnamese.

Loyalty to bad commitments leads to moral incoherence, a syndrome that manifests itself in Christopher's choices of friends and enemies. The epic struggle against totalitarianism for much of the twentieth century was America's Cold War against the Soviet empire. But during the last decades of this conflict, Christopher's platform was the *Nation* magazine—America's leading journal of the "*anti*-anti Communist left"—the fellow-traveling left of apologists for the Communists' crimes, the very people whom Trotsky had referred to as "frontier guards" for the Soviet empire. Although Christopher expressed intermittent internal dissents from this orthodoxy, he remained in his own words a "comrade" of these enablers of the totalitarian cause.

Right to the end, Christopher's political friends were still generously drawn from the *Nation* editorial board and the English Marxists grouped around the *New Left Review* whom he gushingly refers to in an endnote to his memoir as "heroes and heroines of the 'first draft' and of the work in progress."[21] Among these heroes are the aforementioned Victor Navasky, defender of Alger Hiss; Robin Blackburn, a Castro acolyte; and Perry Anderson, an anti-American Marxist who regarded both the 9/11 attacks and the war in Iraq as by-products of the "Israel Lobby's" stranglehold on American policy.[22] Although Christopher socialized and shared political sentiments with a number of conservatives, including myself, there was not a single conservative I was able to identify on this list of political intimates and trusted readers.

As a self-conceived revolutionist within the revolution, Christopher maintained his contrarian ways and kept his double books, avoiding a record as regrettable as his abiding loyalties might have led one to expect. But the record was bad enough. My own experience of Christopher's malodorous service during the Cold War was his presence on a media firing squad that came to our Second Thoughts Conference with the intention of stigmatizing and discrediting the small band we had gathered to announce our revulsion at the slaughter of innocents in Indo-China and our rejection of the destructive commitments our socialist colleagues had made.

Two years later, Christopher attacked me venomously over the account Peter Collier and I had recently published about our second thoughts, which we called *Destructive Generation.* The opportunity was provided when Lewis Lapham, the leftwing host of a PBS show called "Book Notes," invited me to discuss our book on his show and also invited Christopher to comment on what we had written. Christopher singled out a passage in which I had described a small memorial service held for my father in my mother's house. I had written of my distress at the totalitarian overtones of the service, which I felt erased my father's individual memory, making him a symbol of the "struggle" instead. His progressive friends and comrades who gathered for the occasion and who had known him all his life eulogized him as a servant of their political cause but couldn't remember a single aspect of the flesh and blood person he had been. Christopher's comment on this was: "Who cares about his pathetic family?"

Christopher had come to Lapham's studio accompanied by his friend David Rieff, the writer Susan Sontag's son, who lay in ambush for me in the green room for an alleged slight to his mother. I greeted him warmly, not suspecting that he was about to spit at me in a revenge moment the two had arranged. The attack was inspired by a passage in our book, where Collier and I noted the way Sontag trimmed her sails after her famously telling remark that communism was "fascism with a human face," when she allowed the book she had written fulsomely praising the North Vietnamese police state to be republished without revision.[23] I hold no grudge against Hitchens or Rieff for the incident, but it remains a sharp reminder of how fiercely partisan Christopher could be in behalf of an indefensible cause.[24]

A striking elision in Christopher's backward look—particularly for a Trostkyist who regarded the Soviet Union as an enemy—is his failure to note, except in passing, the fall of the Berlin Wall and the defeat of the totalitarian empire. Equally striking is the fact that to the extent that Christopher mentions the anti-Communist struggle of the Cold War at all, his heroes are East European Marxists like Adam Michnik and Jacek Kuron, admirable figures whose second thoughts about communism led them to participate in the democratic struggle against the Soviet state. But contrast this with Christopher's view of the conservatives who led the anti-Communist struggle for nearly four decades. Of Ronald Reagan, the free world leader who actually wielded the power that made the "velvet revolutions" of the Michniks and Kurons possible—or even thinkable—Christopher has this to say: "Even now, when I squint back at him through the more roseate lens of his compromise with Gorbachev, I can easily remember...exactly why I found him so rebarbative at the time."[25] Rebarbative: *adj.*, repellent, unattractive, forbidding, grim.

And what, exactly, might Christopher have had in mind in referring to Reagan's "compromise" with Gorbachev? Could he have been suggesting that Gorbachev agreed not to send the Red Army to rebuild the Berlin Wall and crush the Eastern European revolt in exchange for Reagan's agreement not to *invade* Eastern Europe or the Soviet Union? Can he have actually believed this?

Possibly. For Christopher's text is not finished with Reagan: "There was, first, his appallingly facile manner as a liar"; "he was married to a woman who employed a White House astrologer"; "[he] was frequently photographed in the company of 'end-times' Protestant fundamentalists..." and so *ad nauseam* on.[26] Christopher actually sanitized this litany from its original appearance in the malicious obituary he wrote when Reagan died in 2004, and from which much of the attack in his memoir is cribbed: "I only saw him once up close, which happened to be when he got a question he didn't like.... The famously genial grin turned into a rictus of senile fury: I was looking at a cruel and stupid lizard."[27] This was how Christopher summed up a man who liberated hundreds of millions of victims of totalitarianism and who is revered throughout the former Soviet empire as a hero for this service to the cause of freedom. An Orwellian synthesis of "consistent and integral anti-totalitarianism" indeed.

Contrast this contemptuous performance with Christopher's enduring sympathies for his long-admired but eventually discarded friend Noam Chomsky, a man who spent the Cold War years denying the Cambodian holocaust, promoting a denier of the Jewish Holocaust, and comparing America—unfavorably—to the Third Reich. When Chomsky's extreme views came under attack from other leftists, Christopher actually defended him in a regrettable article that attempted to explain away Chomsky's apologetics for the Cambodian genocide. Christopher called his piece, "The Chorus and Cassandra," as though Chomsky—one of the most cited intellectuals in the academic world—was a prophet of truth to whom no one would listen.[28]

Eventually the two fell out over Chomsky's justification of the 9/11 Islamic attack on the World Trade Center and his opposition to America's military rescue of Muslims in Bosnia. But in his memoir, written nearly ten years later, Christopher still managed to find Chomsky "a polemical talent well-worth mourning, and [a man with] a feeling for justice that ought not to have gone rancid and resentful."[29] As a leftist who had a similar falling out with Chomsky twenty years earlier over his insistence that America was no better than Russia and that *Pravda* was a "mirror image" of the *New York Times*, I can testify that Chomsky's feelings were rancid and resentful long before 9/11, and his commitment to justice was nil.[30]

A similar myopia draws a cloud over Christopher's otherwise admirable defenses of First Amendment freedoms. His long and courageous battle in behalf of Salman Rushdie after the Ayatollah Khomeini had issued a *fatwa* calling for his murder is one of several memorable passages in *Hitch-22* and a pivotal episode in the evolution of Christopher's current beliefs. The Rushdie case was, he writes, "a matter of everything I hated versus everything I loved. In the hate column: dictatorship, religion, stupidity, demagogy, censorship, bullying and intimidation. In the love column: literature, irony, humor, the individual and the defense of free expression."[31]

But in the next breath Christopher fawns over the late Jessica Mitford, a Communist hack who spent her life supporting dictatorships, stupidity, demagogy, bullying, intimidation, and censorship, and calls her one of his "heroines." As it happens, this hypocrisy in Christopher's text has a resonance for me personally. When Peter Collier and I were still leftists, we wrote an article about murders that had been committed by George Jackson and other Black Panthers, who to this day are regarded as progressive heroes. Leftists who were aware of these crimes suppressed the knowledge and withheld the facts in the name of a higher political truth. Peter and I published our article in the journal of a progressive writers' guild and did so at some personal risk, since members of the political gangs responsible for the murders were still active.

While our article was undergoing the usual editorial scrutiny, Jessica Mitford and *Nation* journalist Eve Pell led a campaign to stigmatize us as snitches and racists (since the perpetrators of the crimes were black), and to pressure the journal's editors into censoring what we had written. In a letter describing our article not as untrue but as "appalling" and "atrocious" because it *was* true, Mitford said: "I deeply wish it had never been written." At a public meeting of the progressive guild, to which we also belonged, she told the writers assembled that it was their responsibility as progressives to suppress facts that hurt the cause and to print only those facts that helped it—a practice in which the *Nation* editors are well versed.[32] How, in the light of this reality, was Jessica Mitford one of Christopher's heroines?

Or how, for that matter, is Trotsky his hero? The unsentimental Peter Hitchens observes that the Trotskyist left to which his brother and he belonged was in the habit of attacking Communists in power as tyrants but supporting Communists, when they were out of power, as liberators. As examples, he cites the lionization of Rosa Luxemburg and Leon Trotsky, who, as it happens, were two of his brother's "favorite characters in history" (the other three were Socrates, Spinoza, and Thomas Paine).[33]

Rosa Luxemburg was a revolutionary who was murdered while she was still young and therefore, as Peter comments, "never lived to touch power." Trotsky, on the other hand, became a revolutionary in power and was deeply implicated in the creation of the totalitarian state. He was the commander of the Red Army forces sent to crush the revolt of the Kronstadt sailors, who were Bolsheviks protesting the sinister turn the revolution had already taken in its first years. He was a promoter of the forced labor policies that led to the *gulag* and author of the most articulate defense of the Red Terror, as well as one of its enforcers. He was a champion of the principle that the ends justify the means. How, then, did Trotsky become one of Christopher's historical favorites?

One way was to put on political blinders and focus on the figure of Trotsky out of power—to view him as the author of *The Revolution Betrayed* and the leader of the sect of former Communists seeking to overthrow the totalitarian regime that Trotsky had done so much to create. This, in fact, was how Christopher did see and admire him, although he framed the picture a little more magnificently, portraying Trotsky as the hero of an "epic struggle to mount an international resistance" to Stalin and the totalitarian state.[34] It was as an avatar of the anti-Stalinist left, a movement Christopher romanticizes in his memoir, that Trotsky inspired his adulation. Trotskyism evidently meant to Christopher that he could regard himself as a Marxist and a revolutionary without having to say he's sorry.[35]

There is another way that Trotsky can appear a worthy paladin, which is if one believes that the engine of "history" is still running, and that the epic oppressions of Stalinism were merely an unpleasant prelude to an authentic Communist future. This is, in fact, the way Trotsky's biographer and Christopher's hero (and, as it happens, my own one-time mentor) Isaac Deutscher actually did portray and justify Trotsky in his three-volume hagiography—*The Prophet Armed, The Prophet Unarmed*, and *The Prophet Outcast*. This trilogy was the object of Christopher's intemperate praise in a review he wrote for the *Atlantic Monthly* in 2009. The reason for Christopher's enthusiasm was that Deutscher was a Marxist, and the framework of his trilogy is the assumption that the engine of history is still running.

According to Deutscher, who was writing while the Berlin Wall was still in place and the Cold War still on, the socialist foundations of Soviet society would assert themselves at some point in the future and give birth to an authentic socialist state. This would be the ultimate vindication of Trotsky's ideas.[36] Without such an outcome, there could be no justification for what Trotsky and the Bolsheviks did; for what they did was horrible, and without a liberating outcome would rank among history's greatest crimes. Hence Deutscher's wager on the future. But, as events were to show, Deutscher was wrong: the socialist foundations of the Soviet Union were in fact the engines of its bankruptcy, not the prelude to a democratic future, and caused the system's collapse. Deutscher died in 1967 and did not live to see this result or evaluate his own theories in light of the facts. But there was no such excuse for Christopher, whose memoir displays no recognition of the failure of Marx's theories, or Deutscher's hypotheses, or Trotsky's crimes.

Instead there is the suggestion in Christopher's memoir that "a faint, saintly penumbra still emanates from the Old Man" since the spirit of his "revolution within the revolution" can still be detected in the magical moment of 1968 or in the presence of a handful of Trotskyists in the Solidarity movement, which brought down the Communist regime in Poland.[37] But this is sentimental trash. The "magic" of 1968 was in Christopher's imagination, while an immeasurably greater historical force against communism than the handful of Christopher's favored Trotskyists was an institution that the author loathes so much he doesn't deign to mention it—namely, the Catholic Church.

A better understanding of Christopher's attitudes comes with the realization that he was really more about sensibility than politics, or perhaps that politics was a matter of sensibility for him. Deutscher, a writer of considerable literary talent, made Trotsky into an existential hero, a Prometheus daring the gods. This is why Christopher was enamored of him—because Trotsky was the arch romantic, the incarnation of the lost Yvonne.[38]

The same sensibility underlies his otherwise inexplicable attachment to the tattered figure of Marx. In a conversation with Martin Amis, he said, "For most of my life I thought the only principle worth upholding, worth defending, worth advocating, worth witnessing for, was socialist internationalism." Then he added, "I am no longer a socialist, but I am still a Marxist."[39]

But how? The stab Christopher makes in his memoir at resurrecting the Old Mole to explain the financial collapse of 2008 is merely embarrassing: "My old Marxism came back to me as I contemplated the 'dead labor' that had been hoarded … saw it being squandered in a victory for finance capital over industrial capital, noticed the ancient dichotomy between use value and exchange value, and saw again the victory of those monopolists who 'make' money over those who only have the power to earn it."[40] But this explication can only be tolerated as a literary trope. As economic analysis it is archaic and absurd. *The triumph of finance capital over industrial capital. The dichotomy between use value and exchange value! The suggestion that capitalists are monopolists and make money rather than earn it.* These are themes of a political romance of Tertullian dimensions—belief in an age where God is dead. *Credo quia impossibile est.* I believe *because* it is impossible.[41]

Christopher's comments to Amis seemed to imply that he no longer regarded socialism as a future that could actually work. In an interview with *Reason* magazine conducted just prior to 9/11, he virtually conceded as much. "There is no longer a general socialist critique of capitalism—certainly not the sort of critique that proposes an alternative or a replacement."[42] But why then describe oneself as a Marxist, since Marx's entire critique of capitalism was based on the assumption that socialism was a practical alternative? More importantly, why would Christopher fail to understand that in seeking to achieve an impossible future, revolutionaries become merely destroyers—*nihilists*. If a socialist future is impossible, the effort to achieve one by putting a wrecking ball to existing institutions can only be regarded as malignant and evil.

Notwithstanding Christopher's express doubts about a socialist future, his memoir is laced with unrepentant utopianism. A notable example is his paean to the labor movement, of which he says, "For me, this 'movement' is everything." He then makes this remarkable statement: "Official Britain may have its Valhalla of heroes and statesmen and conquerors and empire builders, but *we* know that the highest point ever reached in the history of civilization was in the city of Basel in 1912 when the leaders of the socialist parties of all countries met to coordinate an opposition to the coming World War."[43]

For those who remember the Basel Declaration, Christopher's remark is a particularly ludicrous triumph of sentiment over history. The opposition to war that the socialist parties coordinated in Basel in 1912 was quickly and notoriously repudiated—by socialists. They had resolved to vote against the war credits in their respective national parliaments and thus prevent the impending conflict. For Marx had written—and "socialist internationalists" believed—that the working classes had no country, and "nothing to lose but their chains." But this was a Marxist fantasy, unanchored in reality, and two years after "the highest point ever reached in human civilization," the same socialist leaders turned their backs on this pledge and voted to go to war. Marx was proved wrong: the workers did have a country, and socialism was exposed as an empty and dangerous pipe dream. The "highest point ever reached in the history of civilization" was thus little more than a memorable hypocrisy.

Although he danced away from his "internationalist" faith and even abandoned his anti-war stance with regard to America's conflict in Iraq, the romantic Christopher still clung to the old fantasy and continued the impossible dream in which the engine of history is still running: "The names of real heroes like [the socialists] Jean Jaures and Karl Liebknecht make the figures of Asquith and Churchill seem like pygmies." And why would this be so? Because, in Christopher's imagining, had an international socialist revolution taken place in 1919, it would have precluded all the nightmares of the twentieth century, including the ones that *faux* socialists like Stalin created: "The violence and disruption of a socialist transformation in those years would have been infinitely less than the insane sacrifice of culture to barbarism, and the Nazism and Stalinism that ensued from it."[44]

In other words, the alternatives mankind faced in 1919 were bloody socialism or bloodier barbarism. Christopher is here paying tacit tribute to the German Marxist Rosa Luxemburg, who used exactly that slogan—"Socialism or barbarism"—to inspire her fellow revolutionaries in 1919. There can hardly be doubt that Christopher still wanted to count himself among them when he wrote these words. Rather than posing actual historical alternatives, however, Luxemburg's challenge was little more than a secularized version of the religious choice between heaven and hell to keep the faithful in line. It was one of the oddities of Christopher's compartmentalized life that the author of *God Is Not Great* and of its brazen subtitle—*Religion Poisons Everything*—was so passionately attached to the political version of an earthly redemption.

In his back pocket, the author of *Hitch-22* kept his own escape clause to provide an exit from the *cul-de-sac* he had worked himself into. The "movement which for me is everything," he wrote, is for all intents and purposes dead—"all gone now, gone to pieces." Consequently, in his mind there were no real world consequences for believing and promoting the revolutionary myth.[45] It was just an idea. But—and here was the hitch—one that for him contained the ever present possibility that it might spring back to life. It was another case of Christopher wanting to eat his cake and have it too.

In the 1970s, Christopher adopted a "second identity," making more and more frequent trips to America, eventually migrating across the Atlantic and setting up shop at the *Nation* magazine. It was another two-track engagement. On the one hand there was the America that functioned as the left's symbol of capitalist hell—a racist, imperialist bastion of oppression. Exposing the evils of his new homeland was the way Christopher earned his keep at the *Nation*, a flagship publication of the pro-Soviet, pro-Castro, pro-Vietcong, anti-American left. On the other hand he was deeply attracted to another America, a land of expansive contradictions and bracing freedoms—which distinguished him markedly from his American comrades. The other America was entirely seductive to the distaff side of Christopher's personality: "Here was a country that could engage in a frightening and debilitating and unjust war, and undergo a simultaneous convulsion of its cities on the question of justice for its oldest and largest minority, *and* start a conversation on the rights of women... *and* have a show trial of confessed saboteurs in Chicago where the incredibly guilty defendants actually got off..."[46]

Would that Christopher had allowed the generous, free-spirited dimension of America, which resonated with the better angels of his own nature, to temper the scorn he poured on his adopted country during his *Nation* years. But the guilty pleasures he experienced in enemy territory had to be paid for by the pact he had made with the socialist devil, and that precluded a just accounting. "My personal way of becoming Americanized," as he explains, "was to remain a blood brother of the American left."[47] Unfortunately, the left that had emerged from the campaign against the Vietnam War was characterized by a corrosive anti-Americanism, which was incompatible with Christopher's otherwise keen sense of America's virtues.

As Christopher became more familiar with his new environment, the increasing irrationality of the *Nation* hostiles started to take its toll. It began with the warm attitudes they felt towards the totalitarian enemy, which did not sit well with a Trotskyist familiar with the depraved nature of the Soviet regime. "I was often made aware in *Nation* circles that there really were people who did think that Joseph McCarthy had been far, far worse than Joseph Stalin."[48] At one point, progressive icon Noam Chomsky unnerved him by saying that America's democracy was morally worse than the Soviet police state. His "much-admired" friend Gore Vidal also jolted him by describing the FBI as "our KGB,"[49] and then by writing an anti-Semitic diatribe, which Christopher protested to his *Nation* editors. Victor Navasky, the editor-in-chief and best man at Christopher's second wedding, decided to publish it anyway, saying, "Well, Gore is Gore."[50]

These conflicts intensified when Christopher trained his sights on Bill Clinton, a veteran of the anti-Vietnam War movement, and the first Sixties alumnus to reach the White House. Christopher, who had met Clinton when they were both students at Oxford, took a strong disliking to the candidate when he ordered the execution of a mentally retarded black prisoner, Ricky Ray Rector, to prove that he was tough enough on crime. The dislike increased with Clinton's continuing duplicity in office and led to a sharp tract Christopher wrote about the Clintons, called *No One Left To Lie To: The Worst Family*. The bad blood created by his attacks on Clinton accumulated to the point where he felt he might have to give up his *Nation* column. "The determination of the editors to defend Clinton's indefensible actions," he writes somewhat disingenuously in his memoir, "completely squandered the claim of a magazine like the *Nation* to be a journal of opposition."[51] But of course the *Nation* wasn't just a "journal of opposition"; it was a journal of the anti-American opposition, and, as Christopher well knew, its audience inevitably gave such hypocrisies a political pass.

Tensions between Christopher and the left came to a head in the spring of 1999, when he appeared before a congressional committee to testify against Clinton adviser, fellow progressive, and close personal friend Sidney Blumenthal. His testimony ended their fifteen-year friendship and inspired attacks from the comrades. It is another telling lacuna in Christopher's memoir that there is no mention of Blumenthal or this matter, which became a minor *cause celebre*. Hence the reader is provided with no insight into Christopher's complex personal and political relationships, or the compass that provided his guide through these uncharted waters.

The White House had given Blumenthal the task of neutralizing potential female witnesses to Clinton's abusive sexual advances by spreading defamatory stories about them to Washington reporters. Blumenthal made the mistake of turning to his friend Christopher as a reporter he could trust to pass on the slanders. Christopher chose to expose Blumenthal instead. In the eyes of the comrades, this betrayal—bad enough in itself—was compounded by the fact that Christopher gave his testimony to a congressional committee chaired by Republican Henry Hyde, a pro-life conservative who was a target of their hate.

This hatred now descended on Christopher's head. Radicals like longtime friend and *Nation* colleague Alex Cockburn began reviling him as "Snitchens" and worse. (Cockburn, with whom Christopher was once joined at the hip, is yet another figure inexplicably missing from the memoir.) In a purification ritual reminiscent of religious witch-hunts, prominent leftists, such as Todd Gitlin, stepped forward to piously declare that Christopher Hitchens would never be allowed to darken their doors again. While Christopher fails to mention his broken friendship with Blumenthal or the internal wrenching it undoubtedly caused him, or the general reactions and the long-term impact they may have had on his relations with the left, he does reproduce one telling message he received on his answering machine. It was left by Dorothy Healy, a well-known Communist and longtime friend, in an archaic argot: "You stinking little rat. I always knew you were no good. You are a stool pigeon and a fink. I hope you rot in scab and blackleg hell...."[52] So much for the warm fraternity of the party of the workers.

While failing to mention the Blumenthal episode in his book, Christopher referred to it in the *Reason* interview, where he recalled how his progressive friends were now attacking him as a "McCarthy-ite" in the pages of the *Nation*. This reaction, he comments, "showed the amazing persistence of antediluvian categories and thoughts on the Left... [which were] applied to me in a very mendacious and I thought thuggish way." He concluded: "There is no such thing as a radical Left anymore. The world of Gloria Steinem and Jesse Jackson, let's say, has all been, though it does not realize it, hopelessly compromised by selling out to Clintonism. It became, under no pressure at all, and with no excuse and in no danger, a voluntary apologist for abuse of power."[53] But in light of the left's long service to the thugs of Stalinism and Maoism and Castroism, was it any different before?

Witnessing the way Christopher's comrades turned on him, I could not help but think of my own experience as an apostate radical.

At the time I was writing a guest column for the left-wing magazine *Salon*, and decided to post an article defending him.[54] "This tainting and ostracism of sinners," I wrote, "is, in fact, the secret power of the leftist faith…. The spectacle of what happens to a heretic like Hitchens when he challenges the party code is a warning to others not to try it."[55] The attempt to purge him I explained this way: "The community of the left is a community of meaning and is bound by ties that are fundamentally religious. For the non-religious, politics is the art of managing the possible. For the left it is the path to social redemption…. [Therefore,] it is about *us* being on the side of the angels, and *them* as the party of the damned."[56]

Like every secret agent, Christopher still possessed his packet of false passports, and he was able to reach a *modus vivendi* with the *Nation* editors who agreed not to print any more defamatory attacks on him, in exchange for what readers were not told.[57] This rendered the purge incomplete, and enabled him to retain a foothold in the left. When a year passed and he hadn't contacted me about my defense of him, I thought he was probably resentful that a political enemy had spoken in his behalf and worsened his case. But then we chanced on each other at a *Los Angeles Times* book festival, and quite unexpectedly he thanked me, warmly and graciously, for the article, and we agreed to make a date for a longer talk. It was the beginning of our friendship. In that moment I also knew Christopher was in a state of motion regarding his allegiances on the left, and therefore, regarding his loyalties to his new country, which he was clear-eyed enough to see was responsible for defending the very freedoms he cherished.

The turn in Christopher's political life would culminate on September 11, 2001, when the United States was attacked by a new totalitarian foe. The threat posed by Islamic jihadists had been first brought home to Christopher when Khomeini issued a *fatwa* against his friend. "The realization that we were in a cultural and political war with Islamic theocracy came to me with force and certainty not on September 11, 2001 but on February 14, 1989," he observed in an interview, "when the Ayatollah Khomeni offered money in his own name to suborn the murder of my friend Salman Rushdie."[58]

Soon afterwards there was another revelation. This time it was about the leviathan the left regarded as the command center of global oppression, but that Christopher now saw as the guardian of religious freedom. The United States military had intervened to stop the genocide of Bosnian Muslims in the heart of Europe when no European or Muslim nation would. "The realization that American power could and should be used for the defense of pluralism and as a punishment for fascism came to me in Sarajevo a year or two later," Christopher writes. "It was the first time I found myself in the same trench as people like Paul Wolfowitz and Jeanne [*sic*] Kirkpatrick: a shock I had to learn to get over."[59]

There were more shocks to come. On September 11, 2001, Christopher was lecturing in the Northwest about one of his personal *bête noirs*, Henry Kissinger, when his wife called from their Washington home to tell him Islamic jihadists had attacked the World Trade Center and the Pentagon. It was the same enemy that had attempted to kill Rushdie, and thus an episode in the same war of "everything I hated versus everything I loved." As Christopher reflected on what had happened, he was immediately torn by two thoughts: the first, a fear of being swept up in an unthinking "totalitarian" patriotism; and the second, revulsion at a comment made by one of the leftwing students who had attended his lecture: "You know what my friends are saying? They are saying it is the chickens coming home to roost."[60]

The remark infuriated him, provoking a response which "came welling up in me with an almost tidal force: What bloody chickens? Come to think of it, whose bloody 'home?'" This last was a telling comment about the loyalties of his *Nation* comrades. When the most prominent among them, Noam Chomsky, regurgitated the same anti-American sentiments, a seismic fissure opened in the ground underneath them: "[Chomsky regarded] almost everything since Columbus as having been one big succession of genocides and land-thefts, [and] did not really believe that America was a good idea to begin with. Whereas I had come to appreciate that it most certainly was."[61]

Christopher began speaking and writing publicly to the same effect, and the more he did so the more vicious were the attacks directed against him from the left. Troubling thoughts began to percolate in Christopher's head: "I could not bear the idea that anything I had written or said myself had contributed to this mood of cynicism and defeatism, not to mention moral imbecility on the left."[62]

Christopher had found a new cause that was not radical and no longer a fantasy about an imagined future but a cause that involved the defense of a flesh and blood reality: "Shall I take out papers of citizenship?" he asked at the end of a poignant post-9/11 article he wrote for *Vanity Fair*. "Wrong question. In every essential way, I already have."[63]

Once he had allowed himself to acknowledge that capitalist America with its passion for liberty and openness to change could be a force for good, other realizations followed. Christopher became in his own words "part of [the] public opinion" that supported America's campaigns to remove the perpetrators from Afghanistan and to unseat the despot and mass murderer, Saddam Hussein, in Iraq. "The idea of 'Reds for Bush' might be incongruous," he observed wryly of his support for the president, "but it was a great deal more wholesome than 'pacifists for Saddam,'" which is what the anti-Iraq War movement supported by most of Christopher's friends had become.[64]

Six months after the beginning of the war in Iraq, Christopher reviewed a book of my political writings called *Left Illusions*. "With the Cold War so to speak behind us," he wrote, "I suspected that Horowitz would find life without the old enemy a little dull. How much of an audience would there be for his twice-told tale about growing up in a doggedly loyal Communist family and his agonizing over the series of wrenches and shocks that had detached him from Marxism all together? But then, I didn't anticipate that in the fall of 2001, I would be reading solemn polemics by leading intellectualoids proposing a strict moral equivalence—moral equivalence at best in some cases—between America and the Taliban. Nor did I expect to see street theater anti-war demonstrations, organized by open admirers of Fidel Castro, Slobodan Milosevic, and Kim Jong-Il, united in the sinister line of, in effect, 'hands off Saddam Hussein.' So I admit that I now find the sardonic, experienced pessimism in Horowitz's book a bit more serviceable than I once did."[65]

While gratifying for the concession it offered, it was niggardly in its appreciation for the battles I had waged and less than the full-throated endorsement of second thoughts I had hoped for. It was one more Hitch-22. If the totalitarian enemies of the American experiment were real, why imply that they were something conservatives like myself invented to prevent life from becoming dull? The suggestion that these threats were a figment of conservative imaginations was, in fact, a standard trope of leftists to deflect attention from their sympathies for America's adversaries. To see

Christopher's ambivalent re-assessment of my second thoughts was less than reassuring.

Only in the final chapter of his memoir did Christopher even begin to address the task of assessing his own political revisions. He framed these reflections as a question about the arc of his career: "Decline, Mutation or Metamorphosis?" By this point in his narrative, there was no mystery that the middle term was going to be the preferred one, and the ends excluded. One of the unkinder cuts delivered in this *envoi* is aimed at those of us who did not regard our second thoughts as shedding a once serviceable skin, but as an occasion to reassess what we had done and undertake an accounting of the damage we had inflicted, and so to make a painful but necessary break from our past. To distance himself from us and avoid the perdition to which his comrades would have assigned him, Christopher wrote: "I didn't so much repudiate a former loyalty, like some attention-grabbing defector, as feel it falling away from me."[66]

Christopher should have known better than to ascribe attention-getting to others, particularly those of us who—because of our opposition to the left—were cut off from the same cultural platforms that made him such an intellectual celebrity. I can't help wondering whether it was fear of losing these audiences that prevented Christopher from repudiating loyalties that helped to seal the fates of so many innocents, as he himself conceded. At one point in his memoir, he quotes Wilde's famous comment that a map of the world that did not have utopia on it would not be worth consulting, and makes this acid observation: "I used to adore that phrase, but now reflect more upon the shipwrecks and prison islands to which the quest has led." Just so. But how, then, could he also speak of a loyalty "falling away," as though it were a matter of discarding some old school ties rather than discovering that he once served a cause that destroyed the lives of millions?

Christopher's unsatisfying attempt to answer such questions begins with the unexpected appearance of his brother, Peter, who had just completed his own memoir, pointedly titled *The Broken Compass*. In referring to his brother's memoir, Christopher singles out a specific chapter that he finds "unsettling." The chapter is called "A Comfortable Hotel on the Road to Damascus," and it is about the dissent of some leftists, Christopher among them, over the Iraq War and more broadly over the "war on terror." As a paleo-conservative, Peter opposed both wars as crusades to change the world, and therefore as endeavors appropriate to the utopian left. "For the habitual leftist," Peter wrote of his brother, the war on terror "has the virtue of making him look as if he can change his mind, even when he has not really done so."[67]

It is a shrewd perception. In Christopher's perspective the war against terror is first of all the crusade of reason against religion and its fanatical believers, which is why he can embrace it without repudiating his progressive roots. The conflict between reason and religion was the theme of his defense of Rushdie. Following the attacks of 9/11 and the publication of his best-selling *God Is Not Great: How Religion Poisons Everything*, it became a personal obsession and the central mission of his work. "The defense of science and reason is the great imperative of our time," he announces in oracular fashion on the final page of his memoir.[68]

But is it? The *jihad* against the West is certainly the product of totalitarian Islam, but it is opposed by believing Christians, Jews, Hindus, and members of other religious faiths. Is it really the case that science and reason are in great jeopardy in the West, as Christopher claimed? It is difficult to see how. Science and reason are hardly the targets of scorched earth attacks such as those mounted against all religions by Christopher and his new utopian allies. There are no best-selling broadsides called "Reason Is Not Great" or "The Science Delusion," nor are scientific institutions being blown up and desecrated the way synagogues and churches routinely are at the hands of Muslim jihadists.

An insight into the religious nature of some leftists' convictions that Christopher offers in his text turns out to be self-reflective: "Rather like our then friend Chomsky, Edward (Said) in the final instance believed that if the United States was doing something, then that thing could not *by definition* be a moral or ethical action."[69] Said and Chomsky took this view because in the Manichaean world that radicals inhabited, the United States was thought of as the center of global oppression, personifying the rule of evil which no good deed could cancel. But is not Christopher's view of religion, as an institution that "poisons everything," identical? Did he not view religion as an institution that *by definition* could do no right?

Christopher's war against religion thrust him up against his own origins. He was not aware that his mother, Yvonne, was a Jew until he was forty-five years old, and she was long gone. The discovery launched him on a pursuit of the past, and forced him into reflections on Judaism, which he recorded in his memoir. "As a convinced atheist, I ought to agree with Voltaire that Judaism is not just one more religion, but in its way the root of religious evil," he writes in a disturbing passage. "Without the stern, joyless rabbis and their 613 dour prohibitions, we might have avoided the whole nightmare of the Old Testament, and the brutal, crude wrenching of that into prophecy-derived Christianity, and the later plagiarism of Judaism and Christianity into the various forms of Islam."[70] This uncharacteristically leaden—one might say totalitarian—prose is alarmingly present in Christopher's writings about religion, and the very opposite of the supple textures and multivalent cadences that normally seduce and reward his readers. "Leaden prose," he warns us in another context, "always tends to be a symptom of other problems."[71]

The problem here is that Christopher views religion generally, and Judaism in particular, through Marxist lenses. He sees religion reductively as the "opium of the people, a sigh of the oppressed," and a future liberation in eliminating the oppressor. Pursuing the cliché, Christopher casts the biblical rabbis as a ruling class imposing their yoke on a passive flock. But this is the kind of misreading of history that ideological formulas inevitably invite. The 613 commandments are not simply prohibitions and are not merely dour. Among many to which one could point, two enjoin the flock *not* to oppress the weak and also to honor one's father and mother. These are commandments that a less ideologically constrained Christopher might embrace. But even if this were not the case, the rabbis could hardly impose prohibitions lasting thousands of years on congregations that did not ultimately seek or need them, or regard them as useful for their earthly survival.

Did Christopher consider how it was that a tiny, dispersed people like the Jews could have survived for several millennia—outlasting all their conquerors—without the beliefs and prohibitions that inspired and held them together? Unaccountably for someone whose mind is at other times so alert, Christopher is blind to the way religion speaks to needs that are timeless and provides comforts that are beneficial, and has contributed to the most spectacular achievements of human culture, including those that are scientific. The very concepts of individual rights and democracy so dear to Christopher are contributions of religious thought.

After the discovery of Yvonne's secret, Christopher embarked on a quest for origins, but his search was destined to end in ambivalence because he regarded Israel, the home of the Jews and the center of Judaism, as an imperial oppressor, and the hostile Arabs of the Jordan as merely passive and oppressed. Christopher's dilemma was poignant. In a conversation he had with Yvonne just before she took her life, she expressed her desire "to move to Israel" without revealing to her son the reason why. It was a desire, Christopher believed, had she actually gone through with it, that would have meant not a personal liberation for her as a Jew, but that she was "taking part in the perpetuation of an injustice."[72]

For Christopher the injustice was Israel itself. He regarded the Jewish inhabitants of Israel as "land-thieves" inspired by a religious myth to establish a "divine claim" and therefore a people who "wanted the land without the people."[73] According to Christopher, in stealing Arab land the Jews became oppressors who "made" the Arabs victims, "with infinite cause of complaint and indefinite justification for violent retaliation."[74] Was Christopher referring here to the creation of a death cult that promises sainthood and paradise to suicide bombers who blow up women and children because they are Jews?

But the premise itself is fallacious, and the passion misplaced. Israel was created out of the ruins of the Turkish Empire, not from an Arab—let alone a Palestinian—land. If a Palestinian state is what the region lacks, there would long ago have been one on the West Bank and Gaza (as there already is in Jordan). There is no such entity because the Arab Muslim goal is not to create a Palestinian state but to obliterate the Jewish one and create a Muslim *umma* "from the river to the sea."

Even disregarding the fact of Israel's origins, consider the war in the Middle East as it is prosecuted today and was when Christopher wrote those words: On the one side, Israel, a thriving, modern democracy containing a million Arab citizens who enjoy more individual rights in the Jewish state than Arabs do in any Arab country. On the other side, a religious theocracy in Gaza and a fascist regime on the West Bank, both lacking individual rights, both prosecuting a holy war against the Jews *as Jews*. "Islamo-fascism" is a term that Christopher was rightly proud to have coined. Is there a single Palestinian faction on the West Bank or in Gaza that does *not* align itself with the Islamo-fascists and their war against the West? Is not Israel's war in the Middle East a war of everything that Christopher professes to love against everything he hates? What was it that bound him to the Arab cause, then, but his unexamined and un-repudiated loyalties to a Marxist past and a utopian future?

Christopher's blind hate towards the home of the Jews was the most troubling of the confusions to which his uncompleted second thoughts led him. The fact that my friend should have been so morally deficient and intellectually incoherent in matters so important— and so important to him—was a personal tragedy and public misfortune.

How to understand Christopher finally? He described one side of his family root as "stern and flinty and martial and continent and pessimistic; the other exotic and beseeching and hopeful and tentative…" This heritage left him "with a strong sense of fight or flight" on family occasions.[75] More accurately, it left him with a sense of *flight and fight* on all occasions, which is as good a summation as we are likely to get. The utopian romance he never gave up was the perfect prescription for continual fight in the present, and a never-ending flight into the future.

Epilogue

I had just completed the above reflections on Christopher's memoir and was preparing them for publication when he collapsed during his book tour. Rushed to the hospital, he was diagnosed with the carcinoma that had killed his father before him. Esophageal cancer is a particularly virulent disease, bearing a short sentence with little room for sanguine outcomes.

Barely a month later he resumed his writing and speaking, leaving no doubt that the sense of irony, which had served as such a notable element of his verbal armory, would accompany him in his final skirmishes. He had been a life-long, aggressive abuser of alcohol and tobacco, although genetics aside these were the principal risk factors for the adversary that now confronted him. In his first article for *Vanity Fair* after his collapse, he acknowledged that he had recklessly baited the Reaper, and consequently would look foolish if he were to be seen "smiting my brow with shock or… whining about how it is all so unfair." But, characteristically, he also proclaimed a romantic defiance of his fate, in a phrase lifted from the poet Edna St. Vincent Millay, in which he described himself as one "knowingly burning the candle at both ends and finding that it often gives a lovely light."[76]

At the time of his collapse, Christopher was the most famous atheist alive, raucously engaged in a crusade to persuade his publics to dispense with irrational creeds and live by reason alone. He had recently taken on the believers in a mammoth best-seller, *God Is Not Great*, which was spiked with acid wit and verbal malice, accusing religionists of poisoning "everything." But when his misfortune became known, the targets of these bilious attacks failed generally to rise to his occasion and look on his misery as their revenge. On the contrary, many announced their intention to pray for his soul and the restoration of his health. In a televised interview, Christopher paid these sentiments a genteel respect, but also assured such well wishers their interventions were useless. He then turned their sympathy into an extension of the conflict he had started, warning them not to expect a deathbed conversion.

When my stricken friend appeared in a video interview a little over a month later, it felt like a personal wound. The chemotherapy he had undergone had taken a distressing toll, rendering him wan and hairless except for unkempt wisps that trailed distractedly from his skull. An unfamiliar slouch tilted his frame, beginning at the right clavicle, which seemed hollowed where the cancer had entered his lymph nodes. His facial skin was sallow and his upper lip pursed as he summoned the effort to push out his words, gulping at intervals for air. I winced at the damage, but Christopher had already turned it into a literary prop, complaining in heroic mode that he had succumbed to something "so predictable and banal that it bores even me."[77]

Who could believe such bravado? Can one's own extinction be boring? Similar rhetorical effects peppered the texts of an article series he had begun about his illness for *Vanity Fair*. In the first, smartly titled "Topic of Cancer," he observed himself clinically, and resumed his crusade against the believers. Reading it, I was struck by how these gestures that now absorbed his waning time and energy were those of a man staging his exit as the terminal chapter in a public narrative begun long ago. The only introspective look he seemed to allow himself in the interviews he now gave about his impending disappearance was when he got around to mentioning his children. The thought of their lives without him, he admitted, made him "moist." When his closest friend, the novelist Martin Amis, was asked how Christopher managed the brave display, he replied, "Not all of you will die is what you think if you're a writer. Because of what you leave. Hitch believes that."

But how could he believe that? Was not Simone de Beauvoir's observation about her mother's death more credible: "whether you think of it as heavenly or as earthly, if you cling to living, immortality is no consolation for death"? And Christopher did seem to cling to living in regard to what he thought of as his unfinished work. Of his diminishing future he wrote, "I am badly oppressed by a gnawing sense of waste. I had real plans for my next decade and felt I'd worked hard enough to earn it."[78] And so he had. But to whom could he appeal this sentence? And to what end, given that he and his potential readers were all bound for extinction?

Judging by the public speeches and interviews he continued to give in his ravaged state and the commentaries he continued to publish, a good part of the work Christopher feared he would not live to finish was his continuing assault on the faith of others, his desire to strip them of their illusions and apparently the comforts they might derive from them. Christopher and I had discussed these matters in the past, and it struck me as odd that he would not now consider rethinking the hard edge he had brought to the subject. "Pascal is a fraud!" he bellowed at me over a lunch we once shared in Beverly Hills. This was his reaction to one of the most poignant souls ever to walk the earth, all because he had hoped for a God to rescue him from the cold night of oblivion. Now Christopher was once again mocking believers for seeking solace in a future beyond the grave. I considered confronting him over this but quickly relented. I could hardly persuade him of the folly of the illusion that he *knew* that God didn't exist and that his knowledge mattered. And even if I could, how would it serve my friend to return his favor?

In the audiences Christopher gave after the diagnosis, his mother's suicide surfaced as a recurrent theme. Although the events had taken place when Christopher was in his twenties, they still gnawed at him nearly forty years later. At the very last, Yvonne had placed several calls from her Athens hotel to England, but he was not at home to receive them, and they therefore went unanswered. "I could never lose the feeling," he told the TV anchor Anderson Cooper, "that she was probably calling in the hope of finding a hand hold of some sort to cling to, and that if she'd heard my voice—because I could always make her laugh no matter how blue she was—that I could have saved her. So, as a result I've never had what people like to call 'closure.'"[79]

Cooper's brother had taken his own life, and he was uncomfortable with the word "closure," which he thought meaningless; there was no end to such a grief. Christopher assented, observing that if there were such an end, "it would only be saying that some quite important part of you had gone numb." As one who has lost a daughter, I can affirm that there is a recession of heartbreak until grief no longer gathers like a thundercloud. But does this reflect a diminution of feeling, as Christopher suggests, or is it simply a resignation to the fact of who we are? Our initial distress is a frantic desire to reverse the event. But the march of ordinary days soon forces us to acknowledge the inevitable and submit to it, realizing that it is not just the one we loved who is lost, but we all are. And there is no escape and no turning back.

"We approach truth," Aristotle remarked, "only inasmuch as we depart from life." He may have had other meanings in mind, but my reading is this: the closer we get to understanding our end, the more we are able to see through the stories that shield us from who and what we are—to see face to face. It was disconcerting to note how little this seemed to be true of Christopher in his final journey.

After the terminal call, Christopher's prodigious workdays became shorter and more arduous. From his own account he was not out of bed before eleven, and he awoke nauseated from the chemicals his doctors poured into his veins in an effort to kill the cells that had run amok. He was thirty pounds lighter and anemic, his skin ashen and riddled with sores, and he faced endless battles against exhaustion in order to pursue his tasks.

These images of a life brutally mugged triggered memories of times past, when I had witnessed Christopher's abusive indulgences and thought: *My friend is killing himself*, knowing full well that it was futile to try to stop him. Even after his collapse he insisted to the interviewers who appeared for his deathwatch that he was without regrets and, even more implausibly, that his addictions were choices whose rewards were so positive that he would make them again: "I can't imagine what it would have been like otherwise… because so much of life to me has been about prolonging the moment, keeping the argument going for another stage, keeping the dinner party alive for another hour."[80]

Braving his way along the last mile, he was still forced to concede that there were moments in which he thought of his children and their futures without him, and it was more than he could bear. Of his youngest, Antonia, who was seventeen, he said, "I cracked up almost exactly the day when I was going to take her on her first college trip. I felt ashamed, depressed and miserable." But when asked whether this did not lead to second thoughts about the reckless course he had pursued, he would not hear of it: "I'd have to say, not to be a hypocrite, that my life is my writing before it is anything. Because that's who I am and my children come later and that's what they've had to put up with."[81]

Harsh words from a dying father, although they were not intended to be an unnecessary wound to hearts most vulnerable, but offered in the way of excusing the life he had lived and was planning to continue. Determined to be undaunted by death, Christopher was busily taking up the thread of the story he had started long ago. Instead of reflecting on final things, he had resumed his mission to change the world. It was his bread of life, providing him the promise of immortality.

Why else would Christopher think that writing was any different from the occupations other mortals pursued that did not save them? In the house of mortality what do the scraps left behind add up to? And why should their production come before those we love, especially our children, whom we have summoned unbidden to a thankless fate and who look to us for comfort along the way?

Christopher's crusade would have been arduous in any circumstances, but it had become particularly grueling in his new existence. Shuffling between chemotherapy sessions and oncology visits, pressing his crippled voice and failing organs into this service he soldiered on. On more occasions than one might imagine possible he dragged himself onto trains and airplanes, crossing the country to slay the dragons of ignorance and superstition. Lungs rasping, he debated one day the existence of God in Atlanta, and denied it the next in Montana, then on to Toronto for a theological skirmish with Tony Blair, the former prime minister of Great Britain. On one day Christopher could be observed warning the public about the sinister revival of the Christian religion in Russia; the next on a radio show sharing his last wishes with strangers, and regretting that he wouldn't live to write the obituaries of evil doers whom he proceeded to name—an African dictator, a former American secretary of State, and the current Catholic pope: "It does gash me to think that people like that would outlive me, I have to say. It really does."[82]

Nor did Christopher hesitate to rub his truth in the noses of the well-wishers who wrote to say they would pray for him, telling them to never mind. "I wrote back to some of the people—some of them in holy orders who are running registered organizations: 'When you say, "Oh pray for me," do you mind if I ask, "What for?"'"[83] (Clever, Christopher, but cold.) Instead of connecting with other condemned souls, Christopher was running through the pages of the last drama he had scripted for himself, whose *catharsis* was a thumb in the eye of death, a martyrdom for the life of reason.

"One of my occasionally silly thoughts is: I wish I was suffering in a good Cause—a cause larger than myself. Or, larger than just the mere survival. If you're in pain and being tortured, and you felt it was helping the liberation of humanity, then you can bear it better, I think."[84] The liberation of humanity. No less. The banner of Yvonne's romantic spirit borne aloft by the loyal son. "Until you have done something for humanity you should be ashamed to die."[85] It was another Hitchens flourish.

In the fall of 2011, Christopher published a thick collection of book reviews and other journalistic ephemera under the title *Arguably*, referring to it as "probably my last." In a brief introduction he explained that he had dedicated his final production to three martyrs of the "Arab Spring." This referred to a series of eruptions in the Arab world that had begun the previous February with high hopes for a democratic outcome but already turned into an Islamist winter, rendering his enthusiasm even more quixotic. After identifying his three Arab heroes, Christopher linked them to a fourth—a Czech who had immolated himself as a symbol of the Prague Spring during the final stages of the Cold War. He concluded these thoughts by recalling a visit he made to Beirut two years before to give a speech to a leftwing audience, titled "Who Are The Real Revolutionaries in the Middle East?" It was Christopher's attempt to fan the fires of an Arab revolution within the revolution, a telling tribute to the path he had pursued with such steadfast loyalty since joining the International Socialists forty years before.

In the speech he praised an anti-Syrian dissident in Lebanon, a political prisoner in Egypt, and a Palestinian critic of "the baroque corruption of the Palestinian Authority"—all dissenters within the revolution, like himself. But the gathering of fellow leftists who came to hear him remained stubbornly unmoved: "It was clear that a good number of the audience (including, I regret to say, most of the Americans) regarded me as some kind of stooge. For them, revolutionary authority belonged to groups like Hamas or Hezbollah, resolute opponents of the global colossus and tireless fighters against Zionism. For me this was yet another round in a long historic dispute. Briefly stated, this ongoing polemic takes place between the anti-imperialist left, and the anti-totalitarian left. In one shape or another, I have been involved—on both sides of it—all my life."[86]

But all his life Christopher had misconstrued this polemic and dispute. The side of Hezbollah and Hamas was not that of an anti-imperialist left but a fascist left. Hezbollah and Hamas were parties of Islamic imperialism and Jew-hatred—as Christopher certainly understood. Why would he even seek an audience among their western supporters if not for the fact that he was unable to relinquish the utopian dream that connected them—perversely—to him? It was the glare of the imaginary future that obscured (and had always obscured) Christopher's political vision.

———

A week or so after learning of Christopher's condition, I decided to publish the profile I had written, calling it "The Two Christophers" after the unruly life he had chosen. Despite the harshness of some of its judgments, I decided to go ahead with its publication for two reasons. First, because my contentions with Christopher over his incomplete "second thoughts" went to the heart of my own political identity and work, and then because I had not given up hope that he might yet complete his own second thoughts or at least extend them. I sent him the article with the following explanation:

July 7, 2010

Dear Christopher,

I hope that by now your doctors have managed to make you feel more comfortable and have alleviated some of the pain you are experiencing. I am told that chemotherapy is an unpleasant matter and I hope that every effort has been made to make this passage easier on you. As you may or may not know, I have written a fairly long piece engaging some of the issues raised by your memoir…. Some of it is critical, as you would expect. When all is said and done, however, my heart is with you. I am grieved that this misfortune has befallen you, and I look to you to pull yourself through it and get on with your journey.

David

July 7, 2010

Dear David,

Sorry that I can't read everything on myself these days (I haven't really even tried Buruma's piece in the *NY Review*) and sorry to tell you that I stopped here with "the

Rosenbergs, Hamas and Alger Hiss." I can't quite think
what made you do that.

Thanks for your kind words on other matters.

As always

Christopher

The sentence he had stopped at was on the second page of the article.
When I located it, I realized he had misconstrued the text, thinking
that I had referred to *him* as an apologist for "the Rosenbergs, Hamas
and Alger Hiss"—which he most assuredly was not. What I had actually written about was his irreconcilable contradictions—that he was
"a friend both to neo-conservative hawk Paul Wolfowitz and to Victor Navasky, apologist for the Rosenbergs, Hamas, and Hiss." Navasky,
of course, was not only his editor at the *Nation* but a close friend, and
one to whom he had given the manuscript of his memoir for advice.
I wrote him an email to clarify the point, and he promptly he conceded his mistake:

> Ah, ok—it was *Navasky* you meant. See, I am not reading
> well enough to distinguish commas from semi-colons....
> No idea what V's views on Hamas might be and don't see
> the *Nation* anymore. Still and all, I think a careless reader
> might have thought you meant me.

I never heard any more from him about the essay, and I don't know
whether he ever actually read it or what his thoughts were if he did.
Important as these issues may have seemed to me, they were evidently
not as important to him. Despite my disappointment over this rejection, it was no more than I should have expected. In the memoir he
had written of his political life he had revealed how deeply committed

he was to the illusions that he had given me the impression he had abandoned. Much as it distressed me to accept this, the path he had resumed after receiving his death sentence confirmed it. Three weeks after receiving his email, I sent him this note:

Jul 29, 2010

Dear Christopher,

I hope you're progressing with your therapy and that its downsides are not too burdensome. I will be in DC Monday evening through Wednesday and would like to drop by and pay you a call if that is something you would like to do.... I have been thinking about you a lot lately and regretting that the timing of my article was so inopportune. I am not proposing this as an occasion to discuss those issues, just a visit from a friend.

David

July 29, 2010

Dear David,

I'd like that very much. Can you try me nearer the time? I have a rather fluctuating condition.

Hope to coincide.

Christopher

We never did coincide. When I arrived in Washington, he was too ill to see me, and then the cancer took his voice from him, which would have made any discourse problematic, and even though it was partially restored he was by then too sick to consider it. I also had to come to terms with his choice to be silent in regard to the issues that had connected us in the first place.

A little over a year after his collapse, Christopher's life came to an end in a state-of-the-art cancer ward in Houston. During that interval I thought about Christopher often, and I thought about him fondly, even though, as I must now accept, Christopher never abandoned the dream of a future redeemed, and of his place in "history" as one who gave a life to achieve it.

CHAPTER TWO

Feminist Accuser

(The Political Is Personal)

Bettina Aptheker is a feminist and Marxist, and also a "spiritualist" who became a devotee of the Dalai Lama without abandoning her radical beliefs. In the 1960s, Bettina joined the Communist Party and was a leader of the most famous campus protest of that decade which took place at the University of California in Berkeley. In the 1970s, she helped to organize the defense in two murder trials of radicals, which were precipitated by an attempt to free George Jackson, a revolutionary felon, from a maximum-security prison. Like many of her political peers, she eventually pursued an academic career and became a tenured activist on the faculty of a major university, where she continued her political work in the classroom.

Bettina's father, Herbert Aptheker, had been the Communist Party's most prominent intellectual and "leading theoretician."

In these capacities he was the Party commissar, an enforcer of its doctrinal orthodoxy. His most notorious service was to write a tract called *The Truth About Hungary*, defending the brutal 1956 Soviet invasion by smearing the rebels (whose leaders were dissident Communists) as "fascists" in order to justify their suppression.

As a young man, Aptheker earned academic credentials as the author of a doctoral thesis on *American Negro Slave Revolts*, which chronicled the uprisings of Nat Turner and others, an expertise that made him the Party's authority on the "Negro Question." When the historic Negro leader W. E. B Dubois joined the Party, Aptheker was appointed editor of his papers and executor of his literary estate. These credentials enabled him to enjoy an autumn celebrity when the Cold War was over, as his daughter's generation of academic radicals secured teaching positions for him at Columbia, Berkeley, and other prestigious schools. Although Aptheker's views remained stubbornly unchanged, his interest in Negro history made him an unwitting forerunner of the ethnic and gender politics that became the fashion for his daughter's generation, replacing the economic Stalinism that was his window on the world.

Bettina Aptheker has written a recollection of her life called *Intimate Politics: How I Grew Up Red, Fought for Free Speech, and Became a Feminist Rebel.* The book provides valuable insight into the ways in which the political is personal for adherents of the radical faith. For her father, she observes, "The Party was everything—glorious, true, righteous, the marrow out of which black liberation would finally come." But the theme of his life was anything but radical: "Loyalty, loyalty to this movement above all else."[1] The mantle he handed down was one his daughter aspired to wear: "To inherit a father's dreams makes you the eldest son. To further his ambitions makes you heir to the throne."[2]

In the Apthekers' household, as in the Party itself, political rectitude required the suppression of inconvenient facts and the shunning of perspectives that questioned its truth. By her own account, the daughter rigidly followed her father's ideological footsteps: "There was a whole world of ideas out there about which I knew almost nothing, because my reading had been so (self-) censored."[3] Before encountering them in graduate school in her late twenties, she was not aware of the work even of non-Party Marxists such as Herbert Marcuse, Walter Benjamin, and Maurice Merleau-Ponty, let alone the writings of Marxism's critics. This admission is even more striking because Bettina had spent the previous ten years as a student and political activist in Berkeley, which had a flourishing culture of radical ideas across the leftwing spectrum.

Generally, the first editorial principle of ideological memoirists is the exclusion of the unruly and the politically inexplicable. For such intrusions might unsettle the meanings of a devotional life. Drained of the unexpected, these politicized reminiscences are not really self-portraits but self-presentations, summaries of the author's postures over time. Eric Hobsbawm's autobiography, *Interesting Times*, is one example of the genre despite the fact that the author is a professional historian. In his text, the personal is all but excluded and there is no glimpse of an interior life. Nor do only memoirs by Communist authors suffer this biographical constraint. The autobiography of Irving Howe, for example, a stalwart of the anti-Communist left, barely mentions such details of his personal life as family, marriages, divorces, and deaths, and how they may have affected his political attitudes and ideas.

The title of Bettina's book, *Intimate Politics*, breaks with this tradition, reflecting the new interest of her generation of activists in "identity politics," and the allegedly political nature of individual lives.

Advance notices for her memoir attempted to exploit this interest by touting the dark family secret its author had chosen to reveal. In its pages, the famously loyal daughter of a famously progressive father exposed him as a child molester. According to Bettina's account, her father, whom she adored as a champion of the oppressed, had forcibly masturbated on her innocent flesh "from early childhood until age thirteen."[4] To conceal the shame, he had terrorized her into silence with a threat that invoked the political paranoia that enveloped their lives. *If you speak out, if you reveal who we are, you will betray us, and "terrible things will happen."*[5] So fearful was the child of losing her father to unseen hostile forces if she spoke the truth, she suppressed what had happened to her, keeping the secret eventually even from herself.

Ten years in the writing, Bettina's memoir is framed by this secret and by its unceremonious revelation to the patriarch at the end of his life: "As I began writing, sifting through my childhood memories, they erupted in ways I would never have predicted. A story emerged. A fault line opened and my world underwent a seismic shift."[6] So she opens the account of her life, closing it five hundred pages later with the confrontation with her father over his unspeakable crime.

At the time of their confrontation, Herbert Aptheker was eighty-four years old and had already suffered a major stroke. Bettina's mother, Fay, who had been Herbert's wife for sixty-two years, had died barely seventeen days before. Yet Bettina responded to a seemingly innocent question, "Did I ever hurt you when you were a child?"[7] with this accusation: *You are a molester and I am your victim*.

"This is worse than Fay dying!" the father responds. The daughter insists: *It happened*. As they go back and forth, desperation overwhelms him. He talks of suicide, and denies the claim. "I can't live with this.... I have no memory of it! You must have dreamed it, or read about it somewhere! I cannot live with this. Therefore, I deny it."[8]

But the daughter is relentless, persisting while the old man, frantically clutching at his own reality, interjects tangentially and even bizarrely: "You know a great moment in history? Nat Turner was in his cell. One arm chained to the wall." This is the trope of a man who has lived his life for History, and is reaching for its myths to save himself. In his mind, all the forces ranged against him are political, or instruments of the political, and he is now one with the rebel slave confronting his jailers who are about to hang him. What Nat Turner cried out to them, Aptheker now cries to his daughter—an image that reveals the grandiose fantasies he inhabited: "Was not Christ crucified?"[9]

In the daughter's telling, the recovered memory of incest is the climax of an odyssey she began more than thirty years before with a discovery about herself: "I don't think I ever would have moved out of the perceived safety in which I had enclosed myself by the mid-1970s had it not been for the fact that I was a lesbian. My strong desire to live my own life—as a lesbian and as a feminist-activist scholar—overrode fear, parental pressures, and Communist imperatives."[10]

The new understanding of her life that emerged from this discovery led to the conclusion that the progressive worldview she inherited from her parents was flawed. This flaw was not in the way it viewed the march of history or the world outside, but in the disjunction between the lives her parents lived and the political views they held. The family contradiction was sealed by the secrets that enveloped them as the agents of a subversive cause: "Everywhere in my life there were secrets. There were those I was told to keep and others about myself that I chose to keep.... [These] secrets kept me isolated, especially from other children, and instilled in me the belief that what went on at home had nothing to do with my parents' political beliefs—those of socialism, peace, social justice, racial equality and civil rights. Of course, I didn't see the contradiction between the way they lived and what they believed until much later, when I realized that I had to live what I believed if I was going to overcome my past and thrive as an authentic person."[11]

But the self-portrait encased in these observations lacks a crucial insight that ultimately prevents her from achieving the authenticity she desires, or emerging from the ideological prison she inherited. This is the religious yearning at the center of her progressive world-view—the desire for a unity of her personal life parallel with the desire for a unity of the world. Thus the memoir that sums up her life is pointedly titled *Intimate Politics*, which is a riff on the feminist idea that the personal is political and vice versa.

In her memoir, Bettina recalls the execution of the Rosenberg spies, who were the martyred saints of her Communist church. The execution took place when she was eight years old, and was "the political nightmare of my childhood."[12]

> After their execution my mother pulled me onto her lap one evening when she got home from work. We were in the big green leather chair in the living room. She said: "I have something very important to tell you." Her voice was soft, almost without inflection. I could feel her breath on my cheek. "Your daddy and I are Communists. You must never, ever tell anyone. Do you understand?"[13]

It was a Communist propaganda point to claim that the Rosenbergs were executed for their political associations rather than their actions as Soviet spies. The politics of the Apthekers were not really a secret since Herbert Aptheker was a well-known Communist figure. But the child could not distinguish between myth and reality in her mother's warning, with consequences that were traumatic when Bettina betrayed the "secret" a year later at a camp for the children of political leftists. Her campmates were gathered on their bunks, boasting about their parents, and ranking them politically. "My parents are Communists," said one proudly. "Mine aren't," another rejoined, challenging the presumptive virtue of the claim. "'My parents are Communists too,' I said. Then I froze. I had betrayed the secret. I was terrified. FBI agents were lurking outside our bunkhouse. They would have heard me. They would arrest my parents...."[14] *Terrible things would happen.*

As an adult, Bettina had occasion to contrast her family's Byzantine household with the conservative family of one of her lesbian lovers. At the time, she was living with a woman named Kate Miller, whose Lutheran parents were visiting the couple. The Millers made no secret of their belief that an "unrepentant homosexual" like their daughter "would literally burn in hell." What struck Bettina was that this did not prevent them from loving her. Raised by Marxist puritans, Bettina had spent decades in the closet, fearful of the consequences of revealing her secret to her own mother and father (and for a long time even to herself). She was convinced that it would mean expulsion from her family and her Party, and therefore her world. Her observations during the Millers' visit were a revelation: "I was most amazed however by their family interaction. The content may have been conservative, but at least everything was out in the open. In my family, everything was communicated by innuendo, and undercurrent, and we kept so many secrets from each other, lying by omission, by denial, by erasure."[15]

The secrets of the Aptheker household were enforced by psychological rages, which terrified their child. "Though my father was passionate and articulate on behalf of causes he believed in, particularly Communism," Bettina observes, "this fire could also quickly turn to unrestrained anger." She recounts a story he related to her about his military service during the war. After the allied troops had liberated Germany, Aptheker found himself pointing a sidearm at the head of the unarmed mayor of a German village, demanding milk for children in a refugee camp. "My father cocked the gun and told him to find the milk or 'I'd blow his goddamn head off.' The milk arrived but my father still regretted not 'shooting the sonofabitch anyway.'"[16]

Her father's explosive feelings caused her to worry that outsiders would regard him as "crazy," which was exactly what she felt when he went into rages at home and when he cried after he molested her.[17] This anger was principally directed at political comrades who had deviated from the Party line. "When I was growing up my father's fury was most often directed against those in the party he perceived as 'renegades'"—those who strayed from the ideological path—or those he perceived as agents of the "ruling class." To Herbert Aptheker, "these men were 'bastards,' and 'sons of bitches,' 'maniacs,' and 'liars.' He snarled these epithets, dumping these men onto the garbage heap of history."[18]

It was her mother's anger, however, that was more immediately threatening, because it was often directed at her. "My mother became furious if I didn't finish my food, but fear of her anger made me too nervous to eat." Fay shouted at Bettina to stand up straight and to stop crying. "Can't you do anything right?" Occasionally parental fury expressed itself physically: "Once, when I was about eight, I was fussing as she brushed knots out of my hair, and she got so angry she hit me on the forehead with the brush. I remember a small trickle of blood ran down my nose. She blotted up the blood with a wet washcloth and continued brushing my hair. She didn't say anything and I didn't dare move or speak."[19]

It would have been one thing if the rules their child had violated were just rules of the house, but in the Aptheker context they appeared as instruments of the perfection that the family sought in its religious quest, which they disguised to themselves as a political cause. The themes of perfection, silence, and rage that dominated the household were encapsulated in a scene that takes place near the end of Bettina's narrative:

> A few months after I started writing the story of my life, I took my parents out for lunch. It was 1995. I was fifty, Mom was ninety, and Dad had just turned eighty.... All through lunch my father sniped at me. I tuned out his mean-spirited jibes about my appearance, my work, my lack of productivity, my children, my political view, as quickly as he made them. The only reason I remember them now is because it was so bad that our waitress, with whom my father had been "joking" in a series of thinly disguised sexual innuendos, intervened.
>
> My father had wanted to order dessert. The waitress said, "I'll bring you dessert if you stop being so nasty to your daughter."[20]

About this incident Bettina comments that she hadn't even noticed the attack until the waitress's intervention: "This was how it was in my childhood. What was untenable was erased."[21]

The Apthekers had recreated in their own family a replica of the totalitarian state: secretive, repressive, sealed off from a hostile world. "This was my own private gulag," Bettina writes, "Stalinism internalized, unmediated, intensified by the madness of McCarthy-ism, and shot through with the terrible violence of my parents' frequent outbursts."[22] The Apthekers' private gulag had its totemic leader in the patriarch himself, whose own perfection could not be questioned: "Looking back now, I know I couldn't have allowed for any memory of my father's 'games' with me if I was going to survive the fear that he would be taken away and the terror that surrounded those times…. In those months, and long afterward, I could hear my father shouting and screaming in the middle of the night as he awakened from nightmares; then I would hear my mother's gentle, urgent whispers calming him down. And then there were those times when he came to me in the middle of the night."[23]

But while she acknowledges the role her parents played in creating the family gulag, Bettina remains loyal to their ideological view of the world outside, their sense of themselves as victims and heroes: "It was a terrible irony," she writes, "that my parents faced the terror of the McCarthy era with so much courage, and yet lined my heart with so much fear."[24] The real irony was quite different. For the "terror" was self-generated. Just as the Rosenbergs would not have been arrested if they had not spied for the Soviet Union, so the Apthekers' political affiliation would not have been troublesome and their political secrets oppressive, had they not joined a conspiratorial party whose alle-giances were to a foreign power hostile to their own country, whose members like the Rosenbergs sometimes became spies.

Nor did the so-called "terror" amount to anything resembling an actual terror. "In fact, my parents were never arrested," Bettina con-cedes, while failing to consider the implications. "My father never went underground, as happened to so many of the fathers of the children I knew."[25] She writes this as though it were another affliction at the hands of their political enemies. Yet the handful of Communist leaders who chose to go underground in 1949 did not do so in order to escape a real persecution, as her account implies. Eleven top Party leaders had been convicted under the Smith Act of running a conspiratorial organization whose goal was the overthrow of the government. The Party read this as a sign that America was on the verge of becoming a fascist state and responded by sending a cadre of leaders to hide in the Sierras and other locations where they could organize a resistance from the underground. But the fascist state failed to materialize. In fact, several years later the Smith Act was declared unconstitutional and the handful of convicted Party members in jail were released.

In other words, the disappearance of the Communist leaders who were fathers of her friends did not just "happen," as Bettina's account suggests, nor was it forced on them by a "McCarthy terror." It was the result of a paranoid fantasy generated by the Party leadership, including Herbert Aptheker, who was among those responsible for the decision.[26] During the McCarthy era Communists were not rounded up and put in concentration camps as Party propaganda claimed they would be. Only a few Communist leaders were ever tried, despite the fact that they were leaders of an organization whose goal was the overthrow of the government, and whose apparatus was financed by a foreign state and included a spy network serving the Soviet enemy. Even now, nearly sixty years later, when these facts are known, Bettina Aptheker is unable to face them. Nor is she able to reflect on the fact that her parents chose to be Bolsheviks in a democratic country and to pledge their allegiance to a totalitarian enemy, or to consider how this might have affected the environment of secrecy and fear in which she was brought up.

II

In 1963, when the 19-year-old Bettina arrived in Berkeley as a freshman at the university, the upheavals of the decade were already underway. She was already a member of the Communist Party, a commitment she describes in these terms: "While I very much believed in the humanitarian, peace and social justice goals of the Communist Party, the Party also represented my extended family, my root moorings."[27] Her parents drove her to California and deposited her in the home of a trusted friend, Mickey Lima, chairman of the Northern California section of the Party, whose home Bettina describes as "a hub of the Communist Party life in the Bay Area." In her book, Bettina refers to Lima and his wife as "Max and Evelyn Martin" (although their real identities did not remain a secret once her book was published). The "Martins" had a daughter only a year older than Bettina.

Shortly after Bettina's arrival she found a place less than two miles from the Martins, and began a romantic relationship with Jack Kurzweil, who would later become her husband. The initial relationship with Kurzweil soon ended, and she turned to a 30-year-old parolee named Raul Hernandez who had spent ten years in San Quentin. Bettina met him through the Martins, who had temporarily taken him into their household on his release. Bettina describes her romance with Hernandez as "enacting a fantasy loosely based on the forbidden love of the Broadway musical *West Side Story*." When Evelyn Martin discovered the romance, she became concerned. Taking Bettina aside she said: "I love you. I want you to find someone whose eyes still have light in them."[28]

Bettina had slept with Hernandez only once, but it was enough to get her pregnant. At the time, abortions were still illegal and Bettina felt she could not tell her parents. In the difficult bind in which she found herself, she was rescued by the Martins, who located an abortion clinic in Tijuana and gave her the $200 she needed to terminate the pregnancy. However, she continued to be friends with Hernandez until he violated his parole and was returned to prison.

Entering her second year at the university, Bettina immersed herself in political activities connected to the Party and gave the appearance of a person increasingly in command. But behind the political mask she was in serious trouble: "Swinging from one emotional extreme to another, I was in a constant state of anxiety," she writes. "Despair dogged me." She drove around Berkeley at night alone, "weeping and suicidal." Back in her room she would sometimes "work a knife into my stomach or my leg as I had done in childhood, now occasionally drawing blood."[29]

She felt herself socially inept, except in her role as a political activist. She regarded herself as "deformed" with breasts that were too small and mal-figured. It had become apparent to her that a giant fissure had developed in the structure of her being. "In the public world, I was Herbert Aptheker's daughter, an organizer, visible on campus. In my interior world, I was lonely, confused, anxious. I felt crazy at times because I couldn't reconcile the two realities."[30]

In this vulnerable situation she began an affair with Max, the husband of the woman whose second daughter she had become. Bettina had come to think of Max as "my West Coast father," and had told him so. The two of them regularly drove together to Party meetings, and he coached her on becoming a future Party leader. But late one night after one of these meetings, "Max didn't just drop me off at my cottage as usual. Instead he came in, continuing the political talk. Then "he drew me to him, kissed me, caressed me." Bettina resisted him, but half-heartedly. She describes her acquiescence in these peculiar but revealing terms, as though she were a political victim: "I became passive, completely passive, the way they instructed us to be when the police came during a demonstration. I went limp."[31] But of course she was not being arrested or subdued by force, and her role—the choice she made in this matter—remains as opaque to her forty years later as it did to her then.

The trysts between Bettina and Max became sexual and continued for a year. "I was not in love with Max; I was not afraid of him. But I felt deep shame about what we were doing, afraid that I would be found out, and that it was a terrible betrayal to Evelyn."[32] And so it was.

Eventually her two clandestine worlds collided. One day there was a knock at her door. It was an FBI man making inquiries. She refused to let him in. It would be a lot easier, the FBI man said, if she cooperated with him. "I will never cooperate with you," she replied, shutting the door on him.[33] This began a reprise of the childhood traumas she had suffered in the world her family's political choices created. "Given the Party's semi-legal status and the continual harassment of Party members," she thought after the visitor left, the FBI must know about her and Max. "That they should know about my most private of shames, that they might use it, made me want to vomit. I thought seriously about suicide."[34]

As the days went by, Bettina became increasingly paranoid about the unseen presence of the FBI. "Somehow we were going to be set up, the Party crucified,"[35] she writes. To protect the Party, she decided to end her sexual encounters with Max. But she felt unable to confront him. The only way to prevail on him to end the affair and protect the Party at the same time, she reasoned, was to keep it "within the family." She decided to ask Evelyn to do it for her, justifying the pain it would cause as a political necessity. Forty years later, she has nothing to say about this decision to sacrifice her friend, patron, and protector, and the Martin family itself, even though the entire drama is a chilling reprise of her own primal scene.

"I blurted it out. 'Max is making love to me.' Those six words were all I spoke."[36] Even in the blurting out, the reality is twisted to make her seem merely a passive victim. Wounded by the disclosure, Evelyn throws her out and cuts off their relations. The deceiving husband denies the affair and tells her: "Evelyn couldn't understand why you want to hurt her like that."[37]

Bettina's failure, even in retrospect, to interrogate herself over the betrayal of her friend is revealing of a person incapable of accountability for her actions and determined to see herself as a victim. "I felt responsible for what was going on between us, *but I knew I had not encouraged him,* and that I had pleaded with him to stop."[38] She had had repeated sexual encounters with the husband of a woman who treated her like a daughter, and continued to do so for an entire year. Yet she describes it as a rape. This *mea exculpa* comes not as the alibi of a confused 20-year-old, but as the considered reflection of a 58-year old professor claiming to have achieved an authentic life. It is a remarkable commentary on her political narcissism that she remains so deeply wedded to the image of herself as a victim, while simultaneously promoting herself as a "feminist rebel."

Months later, the protest known as the Free Speech Movement erupted on the Berkeley campus. It involved the first seizure of a university administration building in what was to become a decade of radical protests, and Bettina was cast in a leadership role. Her emergence in one of the formative battles of the New Left was strictly a function of her prominent position in the DuBois Club, a campus front for the Communist Party. She was the Club's representative on the steering committee of the "United Front" which the campus left had formed to advance its protest.[39] "United Front" was itself a Communist term of art, describing a strategy popular in the Stalinist thirties of forming coalitions between Communist and non-Communist groups. The other factor underpinning her prominence was the ham-fisted response of the FBI and anti-Communist groups who attempted to taint the Free Speech Movement through her presence. As a result she became its second most important personality after its leading figure, Mario Savio.

The presence of a Communist in the leadership of the Free Speech Movement marked a watershed moment in the history of the New Left, which had itself begun as a Communist splinter. Following the Soviet suppression of the Hungarian revolution and the Kremlin admission of Stalin's crimes, many Communists left the Party hoping to form a new radical movement free of the Stalinist taint. But in a famous confrontation at the Port Huron founding of SDS, those who wanted Communists excluded from the organization were defeated. As the post-war "boomer generation" filled its ranks, the New Left became dominated by activists who were ready to forget the crimes of the past, or simply to overlook them. Communists were no longer seen as betrayers of the progressive cause but as victims of a McCarthy "terror."

The term "Free Speech Movement" was a political deception, since the demonstrations were not against the suppression of speech, which would have been unconstitutional, but to protest a long-standing university rule that barred political groups from conducting their recruitment activities on university grounds. The radicals' success in overturning the rule paved the way for activists to turn university facilities into political platforms.[40] The protests also resulted in an end to the requirement that university forums on controversial issues include more than one side of an argument.[41] It was the beginning of the radicalization of American campuses and the intrusion of leftwing politics into the academic curriculum which has had such a deleterious impact on the university culture.[42]

As a leader of this campaign, Bettina became a national figure. Her private dramas would not be revealed until the publication of her memoir, but the disjunction between her hectoring public personality and the confused, self-accusing, and suicidal private self her memoir reveals could not have been greater. Describing her speech to a throng of protesters on the Berkeley campus, she wrote:

> I could not see the people in the crowd, but I could feel their energy. I went through the points I had rehearsed and then I quoted a line from Frederick Douglass: "Power concedes nothing without a demand." A bellow of approval rolled across the plaza. In that moment the crowd's energy surged through me like an electric current. The tension in my legs disappeared. I felt suddenly grounded, strong, uplifted, and so moved I thought I would weep.... The next day I was over at San Francisco State [University] for a noon rally they had organized to support us. When I spoke I experienced the same sense of strength and a deep well of happiness.[43]

Shortly after the Berkeley protest, Bettina married her previous boyfriend and Party comrade, Jack Kurzweil. "Ours was a marriage of mutual relief and refuge," is the way she describes their union.[44] She provided him with entrée into the inner circles of their Communist life. He provided her with "a sanctuary from sexual pursuit, and at least the illusion of heterosexual normality." But the sanctuary proved illusory and there was no lasting relief from the demons that drove her.

Whatever marital life the couple enjoyed was sandwiched between endless meetings about the left's war against the war in Vietnam. Equally consuming was her arrest and trial following the disruptions of the Free Speech Movement. She encapsulates the significant events of this period in a chapter heading: "A Wedding, A Trial and A War." There was also the birth of her first child, unmentioned in this heading as though it were merely a distraction from the tasks that truly engaged her.

While all this was going on, she kept up her secret life of illicit affairs, each of which involved a political comrade and now focused exclusively on women. Martha Kirkland was one of her romantic attachments, an anti-war activist whom she met at the rallies she attended all over the country to support the Communists' efforts in Vietnam. The demonstrations provided the perfect alibi for the husband who was left behind to take care of home and child, as his contribution to the "anti-war" protests. She spent one family Christmas with Martha and Martha's parents in Illinois. On another, she took Martha back to Brooklyn to meet her own mother and father.[45]

This double life caused her to panic at times, when she was overcome with feelings of "self-revulsion." But not because of her betrayal of husband and child: "Once back in my 'real' life in Berkeley and away from Martha, I would be consumed with guilt—not for having been unfaithful to my husband, but for having indulged what I construed as my 'baser' self. I did not know how to hold or balance the contradictions in my life." She sums up her predicament: "I was a married lesbian, having a celibate but passionate relationship with one woman in Berkeley, and a sexual liaison with another in Chicago."[46]

Punctuating this personal chaos were visits from the FBI. Once when opening her suitcase in order to unpack for an anti-war demonstration in Washington, she discovered a pile of pornographic photos on top of her clothes. They were pictures of lesbian sex. Fearful of public exposure, she decided to terminate the romance with Martha, putting Party before self and friends once again, and resolved to make her family seem more "real." She proposed to do this by having a second child with the man she didn't love. Here is how she herself puts it: "I went home to Berkeley and asked Jack what he thought about having a baby."[47]

Through all this, Bettina was still facing jail time for her role in the Berkeley protests. When she finally began her sentence in Santa Rita prison, she was in an advanced stage of pregnancy. Once there, she began bleeding so profusely that she was sent to the prison hospital, where she was raped by one of the prison personnel.

None of these experiences seemed to affect her forward motion, or to direct her attention to other matters, like her semi-abandoned family. When her child, Joshua, was born on Thursday, October 19, 1967, she had three days earlier marched in a violent anti-war protest in Oakland. In the afternoon of the day before she went into labor, she received a call asking her to speak at an anti-Vietnam demonstration the following day. "I hesitated before saying no...."[48]

Though she was only twenty-three years old, her political importance now elevated her to the steering committee of the Communist Party. Of her selection she writes: "I was oblivious to the responsibility membership in the National Committee implied, to the policies we were setting or endorsing, especially in the international arena. All that mattered to me was my personal achievement as heir to the Aptheker covenant."[49] The covenant, which in her mind was her rendezvous with History, had become a scaffolding keeping her from a precipitous fall into the chaos at the center of her life.

In her appearances before campus audiences, she had to defend her Stalinist politics from New Left critics who prodded her about her leadership role in a totalitarian party. Reflecting on these encounters, she writes: "It was a terrible irony that while I was heralded as a leader of Berkeley's Free Speech Movement, I simultaneously justified the Communist suppression of freedom of speech and freedom of the press in the Soviet Union, East Germany, Hungary and elsewhere. I attribute this imprinting to the way I survived my childhood, the sexual abuse in particular: I dissociated from myself and merged with my father, making us one, indivisible."[50]

Ducks are "imprinted," not people. This was less an explanation of her behavior than an indication of her continuing bad faith. Elsewhere, Bettina provides a description of her state of mind and the reason she was unable to detach herself from her totalitarian roots:

> In 1965, after I was married, living in Berkeley, and a member of the Party, my husband, who was also a Communist, tried to talk to me about the atrocities committed by Stalin. Almost reflexively, I shouted at him to stop and became hysterical. I felt that I was holding off a huge wave that would sweep me out to sea and to a certain death. Acknowledging the reality of Stalin felt as though it would crack the structure of my Communist belief system, and with it my loyalty to my father and mother and the world I knew. It terrified me.[51]

This is a more credible account of why Bettina, and others like her who were not sexually abused by a Party commissar, were unable to break with their political illusions. Because their politics was a form of religious belief, to abandon the belief felt like a personal annihilation.

Six weeks after the arrival of her child, Bettina returned to "a full complement of political work." Four months later she was overcome with the symptoms of what she calls a "nervous breakdown." Characteristically, she ascribes the breakdown to the rape in the prison hospital, "the FBI harassment," and the still buried molestation by her father. In a distraught state she cut herself again, apparently with a knife (her memoir leaves the details vague), and suffered symptoms of "acute paranoia" and depression, until she was driven to the point of suicide:

> My mind would spin into a vicious self-loathing: *I am so perverted, so damaged, so evil, I should kill myself to protect others from being contaminated.* [emphasis hers] One day I almost shot myself to death. I was acting out a suicide fantasy. I did not realize that the rifle, Jack's old 30-ought-6, was loaded. I was lying on the floor with the rifle resting along the length of my body. It was pointed at my head. A second before I squeezed the trigger I moved the barrel. The sound of the shot reverberated in our small house. The bullet tore a mammoth hole in the wall of my study. Joshua, in his crib in the bedroom, slept....[52]

As with so many of her descriptions of the traumas she went through, this account leaves the most important questions unanswered. She claims she wanted to commit suicide—but with an unloaded gun. While claiming she did not realize the gun was loaded, she is concerned enough to move the barrel away from her head before pulling the trigger. What stands out as the theme of all her melodramas is victimhood and a passive aggression, against family, friends, and authority. It is this recurrent pattern of victimhood and aggression that links the personal to the political in Bettina's life: "This was my way of working out the relationship between the Marxist (social conditions) and the feminist (women's consciousness and cultures).... I wanted us to stop blaming ourselves for the violence in our lives, the alcoholism and drugs that crippled us and our children, the narcissism and indulgence that sapped our strength.... I wanted us to distinguish between individual failings and weaknesses (for which we can certainly be held personally accountable) and the social conditions of patriarchy, racism, poverty, and cultural genocide that produced them."[53] But if society is to blame for all these problems, even "narcissism and indulgence," what accountability can the individual possibly have? The logic is self-aggrandizing and self-exonerating and self-absorbed.

This same core of self-righteousness shapes her accounts of the role she played in efforts surrounding two failed escape attempts involving George Jackson, a Black Panther Party member on trial for the murder of a Soledad prison guard. Bettina assisted in the court defense of Jackson's lover, Angela Davis, a childhood friend of Bettina's, who was on trial for abetting the first escape plan. Bettina wrote a book about the affair, and explained that prison escapes by black inmates, like Jackson, were analogous to slave revolts, while the indictment of Angela Davis was an attempted lynching—the product of "a frenzy of racist and anti-Communist hatred."

These are the familiar adversary forces that dominate Bettina's political imagination, but the facts tell a different story.[54] George Jackson had been incarcerated in Soledad prison for committing five armed robberies (not one, as Bettina claims). He was given an indeterminate sentence and had already spent ten years in prison before the guard's death, not because he was helpless and black, as she claims, but because he had become a violent gang leader in prison, committing repeated criminal acts, which led to extensions of his sentence.[55]

The political radicalism of the Sixties had penetrated the Soledad prison yard. After meeting Black Panther leader Huey Newton in jail, Jackson joined the party. He became an international celebrity when Newton's radical attorney, Fay Stender, edited his prison letters, omitting passages that revealed his homicidal fantasies (including his plan to poison the water system of Chicago) and had them published under the title *Soledad Brother*, making him an instant hero of the political left. During her visits to Jackson in prison, Angela Davis became his *inamorata* and secretly married him.

The case against Jackson was brought after a Soledad prison guard was thrown over a third tier railing and killed. Jackson and two other Soledad inmates—soon lionized by the left as the "Soledad Brothers"—were accused of committing the murder. They were transferred to San Quentin prison to stand trial.

On August 3, 1970, Jackson's 17-year-old brother Jonathan entered a Marin County courthouse where a trial was taking place involving three maximum-security felons. Jackson brought with him an arsenal of weapons, which had been just purchased by Angela Davis, and handed them to the criminals in the dock, who then took the judge, the prosecutor, and a juror hostage. A loaded shotgun was taped under the judge's chin and the hostages were placed in vehicles headed for the San Francisco airport where young Jackson planned to hijack a plane to Cuba and trade them for his brother's freedom. The plan was aborted when police set up a roadblock. During the ensuing shootout Jonathan Jackson and two of the felons were killed, along with the judge whose head was blown off when the shotgun taped to his chin was discharged.

These facts are uncontroversial and appear in books written about the case by other leftists who were Jackson supporters and who interviewed the parties involved.[56] But they are either obscured or missing from the account in Bettina's memoir because they refute her myth of Jackson's innocence and baseless persecution.

Angela Davis was linked to the case not because she was a Communist or an African-American, as Bettina asserts, but because two days before the attempt she had purchased the shotgun and other weapons that constituted the arsenal Jonathan Jackson brought into the courtroom. Hiding Davis' passionate attachment to Jackson, which provided a motive for her complicity in the crime, was a key strategy of her successful legal defense. After the shootout, Davis went into hiding and became the subject of a nationwide manhunt for months until the FBI found and arrested her. She was charged with conspiracy, kidnapping, and murder.

Even leaders of the Communist Party recognized that these events did not add up to the myth the Davis defense team, Bettina, and the New Left generally were making of it. Behind closed doors, as Bettina relates, members of the Party's national committee wanted the Party "to separate itself entirely from Angela, and a few actually, (privately) advocated her expulsion on the grounds that she was a terrorist."[57] They were obviously more familiar with the mentality and activities of Davis than the white jury that acquitted her, believing her story that while she bought the weapons and gave them to Jackson, she didn't know what use he was going to make of them. To those of us active in the left at the time, the idea that Davis would not know Jonathan Jackson's plan and just by coincidence purchase an arsenal of weapons to which he would have access two days before he was going to use them was absurd.

While the trial was in progress, Bettina insisted that Jackson's crime should be understood as a rebellion of the oppressed. In her memoir, which contains no second thoughts about her views at the time, she describes a Berkeley protest she helped to organize at the height of the furor: "I analyzed Jonathan's action with particular reference to the long history of African American resistance. I drew a parallel between the response of slave owners to slave rebellions, and the modern-day FBI response to these prisoners' bid for freedom."[58] The speech she gave was published in the *National Guardian* and widely circulated. Her father, the author of *American Negro Slave Revolts*, agreed with her assessment: "Drawing on his knowledge of slave revolts and African American history in general, [my father] wrote several articles and spoke at 'Free Angela' events."[59]

Bettina helped to organize the "National United Committee to Free Angela Davis and All Political Prisoners." She correctly saw this political mission as having the added benefit of allowing her to channel the inner rage resulting from her mismanaged life into her public war against America's new "slave-owners." "I threw myself into this work with a passion I had not felt since the Free Speech Movement. In part I was haunted by the memory of the Rosenbergs' execution. Since my breakdown three years earlier, I was still extremely fragile." She was no longer taking the tranquilizers her doctor had prescribed and had undergone no medical therapy. Her therapy was the "struggle": "The intimacy and trust Angela and I developed [in the course of the defense] were sources of great healing for me, especially in my continued bouts of depression and paranoia. I was fighting for Angela's life, but she helped me to save my own."[60]

Though Bettina does not say so, this "therapy" depended on perpetuating the myths of innocence and victimization that allowed Jackson's supporters to sustain their self-righteousness and sense of outrage. How far she and her political comrades would go to re-construe events in order to preserve the myths that fueled their indignation can be seen in their response to George Jackson's subsequent attempt to break out of San Quentin on the anniversary of Jonathan's assault.

In August 1971, a leftist smuggled a gun into the San Quentin facility and delivered it to Jackson. Together with six other maximum-security inmates, Jackson took three guards hostage, tied them up, and slit their throats. As he raced towards the wall to escape, Jackson was shot by a prison tower guard. Unfazed by these details, Bettina characterizes this sequence of events as the "murder" and "assassination" of George Jackson.[61] She summarizes the ensuing five-year effort to prosecute Jackson's accomplices in the brutal execution-murder of the Soledad prison guard as a case "which had propelled ... an eruption of government violence and personal tragedy."[62]

The Communist Party's decision to distance itself from the Jacksons and Angela Davis reflected its leaders' belief that the accused were guilty but also their lack of sympathy as "old leftists" for the new directions younger radicals were taking. The New Left had extended the model of Marxist oppression to other social actors—women, blacks, gays, and outlaws. George Jackson fused these elements in the charisma of a single individual, which enabled him to seize the imagination of the New Left and become its hero. Bettina described the bloody events instigated by the Jacksons as a "watershed in my life."[63]

Her Communist Party comrades, however, still viewed the Marxist proletariat as the agent of revolution, not "lumpen" elements like the Black Panthers and George Jackson, whom they regarded as criminals. In 1976, as a direct consequence of the schism, Bettina was removed from the Party leadership, along with Franklin Alexander, the leader of the "Free Angela Davis Committee." Bettina and Max

Martin were working together again, political pressures having forced their reconciliation. When she protested her removal to him, he patted her on the head and said she was "too individualistic." When she confronted her father, he merely "cleared his throat." To the daughter this was the sign of a familiar decision: Party before family. "What I had always thought was true: I was expendable to him. I could be jettisoned if the Party required this of him." The injustice of his stance particularly rankled because in previous conversations he had agreed with her support for Jonathan Jackson's assault on the Marin County courthouse. "He had shared the same position on the Marin prisoners' revolt as Angela and I had. I felt the Party had betrayed me. I was taking the fall for Angela and for my father, both of whom were too important and too famous to be renounced or rebuked."[64] True enough, but Angela's failure to support Bettina, who had done so much for Angela's defense, was also a personal betrayal—about which Bettina remains silent.

The trial ended in acquittal, partly because of the difficulty the prosecution faced in establishing the real connections between Davis and Jackson, but also because the jury was stacked with political sympathizers for the accused. One of them, Mary Timothy, was an anti-Vietnam activist who became Bettina's lover after the trial.

While the Party demoted Bettina, it refrained from censoring the book she wrote about the case because it had Davis' imprimatur. The Nobel Prize-winning novelist Toni Morrison, who had been a supporter of the Free Angela Davis campaign and a friend of the Apthekers, tried but failed to get a commercial publisher for Bettina's book, which eventually was published by International Publishers, the Party press. A book party was held at San Jose State, where Bettina's husband Jack was now a professor. Angela Davis and Maya Angelou,

another political supporter, were the main speakers. "Hundreds of
people attended, including Mary Timothy and several other jurors
from Angela's trial."[65]

III

After her book was published, Aptheker joined the post-Sixties
migration of the left from the streets of protest to the faculties of
American universities. She signed up for a masters program at San
Jose State in "speech-communication," one of the fields leftists were
busily re-defining to accommodate their political agendas. Other
radicals had preceded her, and were able to offer her an academic job.
It was a position as "a 'graduate teaching associate,' a title they invented
for me since there were no provisions for teaching assistantships at
the universities."[66] Some university officials took a dim view of the
new faculty member's arrest record and the activist temperament
that had led to it and opposed her appointment. Others were "enthusiastic about my arrival." With the help of the Communist Party's
civil liberties lawyer, her supporters prevailed on the administration
to let the appointment go through. She received her master's in June
1976 and immediately began teaching a course on the "History of
Black Women," which was jointly offered by two of the politicized
departments her radical friends had recently created: Women's Studies and Afro-American Studies.

Aptheker's personal life was also moving forward. At the end
of the Davis trial she began an intense but unconsummated affair
with Mary Timothy, a married woman and non-Party leftist who
had been a secret ally of the defense. Aptheker wanted the relationship to be sexual but the older woman, who was suffering from a
terminal cancer, kept the affair Platonic to protect her from a

greater loss. "It was my first close friendship with someone who was not in any way associated with the Communist Party," although Mary's politics were obviously progressive.[67] Her relationship with Mary Timothy introduced Aptheker to the idea that being a lesbian was compatible with leftwing politics, resolving what had been a major conflict.

Two years earlier, her marriage to Jack Kurzweil began to disintegrate. The two half-heartedly sought counseling with a politically compatible therapist. After a six-week separation in New York with her parents, Aptheker returned to California in the fall of 1974, resolved to make her marriage work and to get herself pregnant again. In January, a daughter, Jennifer, was born. But far from turning her attention to making her family work, she accelerated her extracurricular activities. In addition to embarking upon an academic career and entering graduate school, she agreed to become the chair of the Communist Party in Santa Clara County. "I was so busy, I didn't have time to think."[68]

Three years later Mary Timothy died from breast cancer, and Bettina informed Kurzweil that she was divorcing him. They had been married for thirteen years. "When I asked Jack for a divorce in February 1978, three weeks after Mary's death, he started to cry. By this time I was too angry to allow other emotions to emerge. A steel door had closed over my heart."[69] It does not appear from her account of these events that her anger had anything to do with her husband, or that the decision to leave him was the consequence of any change in their relationship or any action on his part. The death of the woman she loved was the apparent catalyst. She sums up her decision to break up her family in these words: "We had been married for thirteen years, and I felt like my life was just beginning. I didn't know if I could live openly as a lesbian, but I was alive with new ideas, caught up in the strength of the women's movement."[70] Once again, she had sacrificed her family for the cause.

In graduate school, Bettina had begun for the first time in her life to open her mind to the work of leftwing writers who were not on the Party's list of approved authors. At the same time, she was careful to limit the range of her interest to the writings of authors who were politically correct by the standards of her New Left comrades: "radical feminists, authors who applied a Marxist paradigm to gender issues," and those approved by the Women's Studies movement such as Shulamith Firestone and Juliet Mitchell, authors of *The Dialectics of Sex* and *Women: The Longest Revolution*.[71] In the new orthodoxy she had embraced, a mythical "patriarchy" took precedence over the Marxist ruling class as the well-spring of social evils. In the radical vision she now adopted, women took their place beside the proletariat as a fundamental element in the axis of social "oppression" and thus in the revolutionary struggle for "social justice."

The Women's Studies class she taught was called "Sex and Power," and its agenda was to instill in her students the new doctrines she had just embraced: "We had long discussions about sexism in language, about how women were oppressed as a group, about how violence affected women's lives, and about race and class as part of interconnected systems of domination."[72] She had found a way to integrate her ideological existence with the sexual longings she had kept so long in the closet of her secret life. And in the university she had found a new platform for her political mission.

The timing could not have been more propitious. The entrenchment of radicals in academic departments like Women's Studies had advanced far enough to offer her a career through which she could financially support her new independence and carry on her Communist political work. She applied for a job at the University of

California, Santa Cruz, and also in Stanford University's radicalized Education Department. Both faculties liked her attitude and provided her with "very generous financial offers for scholarships and employment," but Santa Cruz was her choice.[73] Without fully realizing its implications, she had in effect joined a new radical party, one that allowed her to integrate her political and professional careers.

The Santa Cruz region, south of San Francisco, was an area she was particularly attracted to because of its large lesbian community. In her interview at the university she discovered just how radicalized it had become and how distant from the traditional academic procedures she was used to: "This process was striking in the way it put collective and non-hierarchical politics into practice."[74]

To pursue a university career she would need a credential, so she enrolled in the "History of Consciousness" graduate program. Her political alter ego, Angela Davis, was already a professor on the faculty of the program, and the department was so attuned to her radical politics that it had awarded Huey Newton, the cocaine-addicted felon and Black Panther leader, a doctorate. To qualify for the degree, Newton had submitted a self-serving political tract titled, "War Against the Panthers: Repression in America." Aptheker herself describes the "History of Consciousness" major as "an interdisciplinary program with an emphasis in twentieth century radical and Marxist philosophies."[75]

The academic quality of the "History of Consciousness" curriculum in Marxism can be gauged by Aptheker's account of the program after she had entered it: "I was one of only two or three students in our seminar who had actually read Marx, and I became a sort of expert-in-residence. Everyone, even [Professor] Hayden White and [Professor] Jim [Clifford], seemed to find Marx either indecipherable or to reduce his work to purely economic terms—that is, that Marxism could explain the exploitation of the workers in basic industry and how profits were made, but not much else."[76] So the student novice became the instructor of her professors—evidently inexpert in their own field—in Marxist truths. The politicized curriculum suited her: "I was not interested in learning one more time what I saw as the patriarchal lineage of American historians." In a statement of purpose the department required her to file in order to be accepted into the program, she explained that she wanted to "t/ease [sic] the juxtaposition of Marxism and feminism into a unified theory of liberation."[77]

Her quest for a unified path to social and personal liberation inevitably set her on a collision course with her tradition-bound father and his Party. Her book on the trial of Angela Davis had been the most popular title for International Publishers, the official Party press, and her editor wanted another. She offered him a collection of pieces, which she called *Woman's Legacy: Essays on Race, Sex and Class in American History.* It was a contribution to her new radical enterprise: "In writing *Woman's Legacy* I was, in fact, seeking to put Marxism and feminism into a unified theory of oppression and liberation—just as in my graduate school I'd said I'd hoped to do.... By this time... I no longer saw class as the principal or only instrument of oppression upon which all others rested. I was working out ideas about systems of domination based on race, sex, and class which were interdependent and interlocking."[78] What she was "working out" was in fact the emerging ideological formula ("the intersection of race, class and gender") of Women's Studies Departments across the country.

Aptheker's book, *Woman's Legacy*, was neither an academic inquiry nor a theoretical treatise. It was a series of party polemics— often quite crude—about race, sex, and class. The substance of these polemics was standard Communist fare, drawing mainly on writers who were Party approved, its arguments reflecting the coarse syntax of the Party's engagements with its opponents. One of Aptheker's chapters, for example, was about the famous Moynihan Report on the plight of the black family, which was written by the distinguished social scientist Daniel Patrick Moynihan for the liberal administration of Lyndon Johnson. Basing his conclusions on the historical experience of the Irish in America, Moynihan had presciently warned that the rising out-of-wedlock births in lower class black communities and lack of fathers present in the home would have serious social repercussions.

Aptheker did not actually examine or discuss the detailed analysis of the Moynihan Report or the data he assembled. Instead she attacked what she regarded as its reactionary implications. For example, she condemned its observations about the importance of fathers in the home as a call "for the introduction of patriarchal relations in the Black community" and described Moynihan's observations in terms reminiscent of her father's brutal polemics: "The Moynihan doctrine was neither a historical accident nor the innocent blunder of a stupid man. It represented a necessary judgment in racist/male supremacist ideology to correspond to the actual shift of Black women in society."[79]

In writing the book's sixth chapter on domestic labor, Aptheker realized she might have a problem. "I could not hold on to the orthodox formulations of Marxism and still see women as the co-equals of men in the making of history." Pursuing her new feminist interests, she had come to the conclusion that Marx and Engels were "sexists." Her task was to make them feminists: "Those of us working to bring Marxism and feminism together in theory argued that ... household labor may have had a loving aspect, but it also made possible the *re*-production of the working class upon which the whole economic system of capitalism depended. This constituted, we argued, a *co-equal* form of exploitation"[80] (emphasis hers).

Just before Aptheker's book was sent to press, she received a two-and-a-half-page letter from a member of the Party's "National Commission on Women," which informed her, "It is clear that you have developed some basic differences with the Party, and I should add, with Marxist-Leninist theory, on the source and nature of women's oppression under capitalism."[81] It is a testament to her continuing ideological myopia and inability to view herself at any distance that Aptheker should be shocked to learn—the year was 1979—that the Communist Party might censor views it regarded as doctrinally impure: "I was in complete turmoil over her letter. I had expected controversy over the chapter on domestic labor, but I had not expected a broadside like this, which dismissed all of the research I had done and decreed what constituted Marxism-Leninism."[82]

It is difficult to understand how such a sentence could be written. After all, Communist parties had been conducting purges of those who strayed from their decrees ever since their creation. This was the political tradition Aptheker was born into and had thrived in, and whose strictures she herself had enforced. Yet despite her self-conceived strides towards "liberation," at the age of thirty-seven she was stunned to discover that Communists would enforce their party line against *her*.

Again she "felt a sense of overwhelming betrayal by my Party," which threw her into "the worst psychological state I'd been in since my nervous breakdown at twenty-three."[83] In this crisis, her father was generous in his support, announcing that he would never publish another book under the Party imprint. She acknowledges that this was "an extraordinary gesture."[84]

A year later, on October 12, 1981, she resigned from the Party. But she did not disclose she had done so for another year because she feared that a public announcement might give aid and comfort to the enemy camp. As for any good Communist, the enemy was her own country. She wanted to avoid a gesture that might be interpreted as a protest against the Soviet Union,[85] and did not want to be perceived as "hostile to the Communist Party," or a "renegade"—a class of individuals reviled by her father and her political friends. She regarded herself as "still a revolutionary. A good person."[86]

On hearing the news of his daughter's break with the Party, Herbert Aptheker became semi-hysterical, shouting at her as he had never done before, until his wife intervened, "Herbert that's enough." Then, in what his daughter describes as a voice hoarse with regret, he said: "The Soviet comrades will never understand it. Never!" To Bettina, "it sounded crazy. Why would the Soviet comrades care about what I did?"[87] But of course what they cared about was Herbert Aptheker, the Party's "leading theoretician," who could not keep his own daughter in line.

Woman's Legacy—the ideological tract the Party rejected—was immediately bought by the University of Massachusetts Press, whose director, Leone Stein, was a friend of Herbert Aptheker and had overseen the publication of his edition of the correspondence of W. E. B. DuBois. Such was the transformation of American universities then taking place that the same political tract that destroyed her Party career now became a stepping-stone towards academic tenure. Notwithstanding the fact that her book was only a collection of political broadsides, it was sufficient for Hayden White, who was a member of her dissertation committee in the History of Consciousness program. White proposed that she submit it as her doctoral thesis, which she did.[88]

With a Ph.D. under her belt, she now possessed the credential required to take her place as a full member of a university faculty. Even better, her political allies on the faculty now placed her in a position to shape the emerging Women's Studies program at Santa Cruz, a pioneer program in Women's Studies nationally that had not yet secured approval as a full-fledged department. As her first teaching assignment, she was offered the primary course, "Introduction to Women's Studies," which until then had been taught by another Berkeley Marxist, Barbara Epstein.

Employing her blunt instrument approach to all things intellectual, Bettina converted her class of undergraduates into a political cell meeting: "I redesigned the curriculum and retitled it, 'Introduction to Feminism,' making it more overtly political, and taught the class in the context of the women's movement." Most of her students "were activists themselves."[89] Nothing remotely academic or scholarly entered her lesson plan: "Teaching became a form of political activism for me, replacing the years of dogged meetings and intrepid organizing with the immediacy of a liberatory practice."[90]

Throughout the 1980s, the Women's Studies program at UC Santa Cruz lacked the status of an official department and had to depend on courses that were taught by faculty radicals with positions in other liberal arts disciplines. Then, in 1986, Bettina was offered a position as the university's first Women's Studies professor. She hesitated, if only briefly, before accepting the post because of the actual academic responsibilities it might entail. "I was not sure I wanted a tenure track position at the university with all that that implied about serving on faculty committees, publishing under pressure and attending scholarly conferences." But her radical faculty sponsors prevailed on her. Marge Frantz, a lecturer in American studies and, like Aptheker, a former Bay Area Communist, advised her: "It's your revolutionary duty!"[91] This was persuasive, and she took the job. In 1996, after an intense campaign of protests, which Aptheker helped to organize, administrators caved in to the political pressures and approved the creation of a Women's Studies Department. Under the prodding of Aptheker and her allies, it was subsequently re-named the Department of Feminist Studies.

While Aptheker was re-formulating her political agenda, she was also re-shaping her personal odyssey in a manner she describes in these terms: "Now that I had broken from the Party and [therefore] from [my father], I needed another person with whom to merge."[92] Merging is an odd but particularly revealing way for someone to describe a momentous step in a lifelong pursuit of "liberatory" ends. The new authority figure in her life was a mid-westerner named Kate Miller, who became her live-in mate and guide. Miller was also a Buddhist, and soon led Aptheker into a new authoritarian community to replace the one she had just left, this one headed by the Dalai Lama.

The most powerful impulse of the totalitarian mind is the passion for a unity of society—the passion to merge. It is the passion for a unity that will resolve all conflicts, and establish social harmony, and internal peace. It is this drive for unity that leads inexorably to the obliteration of individuals and their messy and unruly truths. Even at this late stage, Aptheker remained ideologically straight-jacketed, unable to free herself from the terrible legacy of the cause she and her family had served.

"I was almost knocked off my feet by the power of the energy that the Dalai Lama was generating," Aptheker writes of the appearance of the god-in-man at an event she attended in the San Jose Sports Arena. During the high point of the ceremony, the Dalai Lama disappeared into the universe and was no longer an individual: "He was no longer the Dalai Lama or anyone; he was just an energy field. I looked over at Kate to see her stagger a step or two before regaining her balance. We were both crying."[93] It was the annihilation of self— the moment she had longed for all her life.

Along with its vision of redemption, Buddhism delivered a practical technique for releasing her anger. "I was always denying that I was angry. The process that would work to release anger was not denial and repression, but acknowledgement and dissolution.... To dissolve my anger meant to forgive; to forgive meant to practice compassion."[94] So much for the sermon. What this compassion meant to her in practice is revealed in her account of the confrontation with her 84-year-old father over the buried family secret.

For this confrontation she chose an occasion seventeen days after the death of her mother, who had been Herbert's wife for sixty-two years. Life-long rage once again had made her oblivious to the human context of her actions. Having denied his daughter's accusation, the father asked how she could forgive him if it were true. "I said, 'I have already forgiven you.' And it was true. In those few minutes his anguish had been so palpable that all of my anger had dissolved. Because, of course, I loved him. What arose for me in that moment in the car was a compassion so vast, so limitless that it embraced not only my father, but every being in the world."[95]

Was this the daughter speaking? Or the Buddhism? A compassion that embraces every being in the world embraces no being in particular, something the wounded target of her anger would understand. Aptheker's Buddhism was not about compassion; it was about her narcissism, the endless embrace of the self-justifying self. In discussing the five vows of a bodhisattva (not to kill, not to steal, to avoid sexual misconduct, to avoid telling lies, and to avoid drugs and alcohol), she observes that didn't realize how hard they would be to keep. It leads her to this reflection: "I finally realized that the oath like the precepts and perfections was not about having an objective standard by which to judge one's actions; rather, it was about having an internal standard for one's own motivations."[96] In other words, good intentions were enough.

Aptheker's oaths were not binding commitments to others. They were about excusing herself, because she meant well. Which is, in the end, what her account of her life is about, and also her political radicalism. The self is not accountable. It is others—Society—that are to blame. Did she have bad politics and defend awful crimes? Her love for her father made her do it. Did she betray and brutalize her father when he was old, and defenseless, and alone? Her father brutalized her and she forgave him because she loved him as she loved and forgave all beings.

After a life toiling in the vineyards of the totalitarian left, Aptheker's marriage of class politics and identity politics and spiritual politics—her unified theory of liberation—is finally incoherent. Towards the end of her memoir, she offers her new understanding of the failure of the socialist utopia to which she had dedicated the bulk of her years—a failure that is otherwise hardly referred to in this lengthy account of her radical life:

> From my experience in East Germany and at the Berlin Wall, the failure of socialism seemed no great mystery to me. Socialism had failed because of the corruption of those who led it, and those who had lived under it.... I no longer believed that you could legislate altruism, which is part of what Communist governments had tried to do, according to their own formulas for social justice. Greed and jealousy, anger and hatred, power and revenge were

all inherent to the human condition. Unless political action was combined with internal development to produce true compassion, it would always be seriously if not fatally compromised.[97]

But what is the purpose of the political action that Aptheker has spent her whole life pursuing if human suffering is caused by the moral flaws in individuals that are "inherent to the human condition," which millennia of religious missions and political isms have failed to change?

In fact, in spite of her spiritual protestations, Aptheker is as wedded at the end of the life as at the beginning to the totalitarian passion she inherited from her father. At a rally on the Santa Cruz campus to protest America's effort to prevent the tyrant Saddam Hussein from swallowing Kuwait during the first Gulf War, Aptheker was a featured speaker:

I used the occasion to test a way to combine my feminist, Marxist, and spiritual ideas. I began by conjuring the image of George Bush and Saddam Hussein as two patriarchs gearing up for war, testing their manhood like medieval knights in full body armor, wielding their mighty lances, swinging mindlessly at each other. I said it would be funny if not for the thousands and thousands of women, children, and men who would die as a consequence. I talked in some detail about the oil companies, their corporate priorities and imperial interests. I said this was not a war about freedom and democracy; it was about power and greed, and the continuation of U.S. domination in the region. With the Soviet Union gone, the United States had no military opposition with which to reckon.[98]

Herbert Aptheker could not have said it better. His daughter had merely bottled the old wine in a new container: "I called upon each of us to strive toward inner peace.... I urged us to model ourselves after the Buddha.... It felt different to talk about the war in this way." It probably did. But inciting her students to hate their own country as an imperialist demon was not. Venting her personal rage on external forces and serving America's enemies was to do what she had always done, and be what she had always been.

CHAPTER THREE

Cultural Decline

"Cornel is, quite simply, the leading public theologian of our age."
—Serene Jones, president, Union Theological Seminary, 2011

C ornel West is an icon of the intellectual culture. He is an academic star who sat on the faculties of Harvard, Princeton, and Yale before finding a home at the Union Theological Seminary in New York. He was named to the Council of Black Advisers of Barack Obama's presidential campaign and in 2007 introduced the future White House occupant on his first stop in Harlem, where West referred to him as "my brother and my companion and comrade." Obama reciprocated by calling West "not only a genius, a public intellectual, an oracle ... [but] also a loving person."[1] West had previously campaigned for former president Bill Clinton, and was political adviser to Senator Bill Bradley and to the Reverend demagogue Al Sharpton in their failed bids for the Democratic Party nomination during the 2004 primaries.

In addition to tenured appointments (and six-figure incomes) at four elite American schools, West has also taught at the University of Paris. He has been awarded twenty honorary university degrees and is the author of nineteen published books, two of which made the *New York Times* best-seller list with over 100,000 hardcover copies sold. He is one of a handful of living authors included in the curriculum of Columbia University's great books program, and there are more references to his work in academic professional journals than to fourteen other specially honored "University Professors" on the Harvard faculty. References to his work by other professors number twice those of Harvard's former president, Larry Summers, a distinguished academic, secretary of the Treasury in the Clinton administration, and chairman of the White House Council of Economic Advisors under Barack Obama.[2]

A rancorous quarrel between West and Summers erupted shortly after the 9/11 jihadist attacks, when the Harvard president questioned West's scholarly record and commitment. West prevailed when their confrontation led to an unprecedented censure of Summers by his own faculty. West was then promptly recruited for a prestigious post at Princeton. The affair was considered a momentous cultural event by the *New York Times*, which reported the conflict on its front page, alongside the national news.

A tireless self-promoter, West habitually refers to himself and his work as "prophetic" (e.g., "I am a prophetic Christian freedom fighter"), and has put the words "prophetic" or "prophesy" in the titles of four of his books, including a collection of casual pieces and book reviews he called *Prophetic Fragments*, as though Ezekiel was his soul mate and the parchments containing his wisdom had been eaten by the sands of time.[3]

A man of vaudevillian dimensions, who is known affectionately to friends as "Corn," West's self-adulation is infectious to others and has inspired a chorus of prominent enablers. Pulitzer Prize-winning author Maya Angelou testifies: "Cornel West thinks like a sage, acts like a warrior and writes like a poetical prophet." Marian Wright Edelman, friend of Hillary Clinton and head of the Children's Defense Fund, concurs: "Cornel West is one of the most authentic, prophetic and healing voices in America today."[4] *Newsweek* describes him as "an eloquent prophet," while *Time* lauds him as a "brilliant scholar,"[5] although he has not produced an academic work in more than twenty years—one of the bones of contention between him and the president of Harvard. Guardians of the higher culture have joined the promotion. When conservative critics questioned West's intellectual credentials, the editor of the *New York Times Book Review*, Sam Tannenhaus, defended him: "West has a Ph.D. in philosophy from Princeton, and his work has been explicated by, among others, Harvard philosopher Hilary Putnam.... West is, moreover, a master of intellectual exchange."[6] He is also probably the only professor currently on a faculty who has had a school named after him—the oxymoronic Cornel West Academy of Excellence in Raleigh, North Carolina.[7]

The fan club West has acquired is not limited to his native shores: "What a blessing it was," he writes,

> to deliver the Edward Said Memorial Lecture in Cairo Egypt, the Nelson Mandela Lecture in Pretoria, South Africa, the UNESCO Lecture in Santiago, Chile, and the Albert Einstein Forum Lecture in Berlin, Germany.... I like seeing [my book] *Race Matters* translated into Japanese,

Italian, and Portuguese. I like seeing [my book] *The American Evasion of Philosophy* translated into Chinese, Spanish and Italian. I like that there are hundreds of thousands of copies of my book *Democracy Matters* translated into Spanish.... I like the fact that all nineteen of my books are still in print with the exception of the two that won the American Book Award in 1993.... I like the fact that seven insightful books, both scholarly and mainstream have been published on my life and work.[8]

He is also the object of *homages* from the popular culture:

I like the fact that the beautiful "Cornel West Wall" exists on Martin Luther King Boulevard in Trenton, New Jersey. I am grateful for the illustrious talent of artist Luv One [who painted it].... I like that the remarkable young hip-hop artist Lupe Fiasco [*sic*] has honored me by naming his Grammy-nominated album *The Cool* after a lecture I gave in Chicago.... I like performing with those bebop jazz giants, the Heath Brothers ... I like that on my most recent CD, *Never Forget: A Journey of Revelations*, I collaborated with outstanding artists like Talib Kweli, KRS-One, Jill Scott, Andre 3000, and Cliff West [his brother]. I was delighted to be named MTV Artist of the Week and gratified when the album hit the Billboard charts: #1 Spoken Word and #37 R&B/Hip Hop. I like the thrill of collaborating with the incomparable musical genius of our time, Prince.... I like that these days more people recognize me from my little movie roles than my books.... Ironically, I made my film debut in *The Matrix Reloaded*, the movie

that broke all existing box office records.... I've performed
in films such as ... *The Private Lives of Pippa Lee*, directed
by Rebecca Miller (daughter of my dear brother, the late
great Arthur Miller)....[9]

Who is this man who has been elevated to such prominence by cultural arbiters high and low? His newly published autobiography,
Brother West: Living and Loving Out Loud (and don't even attempt to
parse that title), answers the question with an epigraph, which is a
citation from himself:

> *"I'm a bluesman in the life of the mind, and a jazzman in
> the world of ideas."* —Cornel West

Like many sentences West writes, this catchy phrase is a substitute
for thought that does not make any sense. "But what does it mean to
be a bluesman in the life of the mind?" The answer: "I try to give heart
to the intellect by being true to the funk of living. For me this can
only be seen through the lens of the cross and realized in the light of
love." And this means? "I greet each person struggling through time
and space in search of love and meaning before they die as brother
or sister no matter what their color."[10]

The eighteenth-century essayist Joseph Addison once said that he
believed in ghosts "in the general but not in the particular." So West's
love is distributed indiscriminately among strangers and intimates
alike. Even my used copy of *Living and Loving Out Loud* is auto-
graphed to no one in particular: "Love, Cornel West." Perhaps that is
what Obama meant when he described West as "a loving person." Not
surprisingly, West's personal life is a perfect chaos. He has fathered
children with three different women dispersed on three continents.

Even his estranged American wife and child reside a thousand miles distant from his home. It hardly takes a Freudian to suspect that the oceanic love he expresses towards strangers is a displacement of the desire for the human connection that has proved so elusive for him.

But even this abstract love turns out to be a posture. Not everyone is actually the object of his affectionate vapors, particularly those who stand in the way of his radical designs or his personal ambitions. West damns Harvard's liberal president as a liar and a racist, and Summers is but one in the numerous company of "racists," "sexists," "homo-phobes," and "Islamo-phobes" who are recurring targets of West's indictments, along with a society that has bestowed on him so many undeserved privileges and honors.

He was a celebrity sponsor of the 2012 "Global March to Jerusa-lem," an attack organized by Islamist Iran on the Jewish state.[11] He has been a frequent speaker at the black liberation church of another sponsor of the Global March, Jeremiah Wright, the notorious anti-Semite and race-hater whom West regards as "my dear brother" and "a prophetic Christian preacher." West defends the infamous Wright anathema—"God *damn* America"—explaining that it is the function of prophetic Christians like Wright to call on God *to* damn America, because America is no different from every nation that treats its citizens as "less than human."[12]

As an academic celebrity, West is annually invited to deliver more than a hundred speeches on university campuses at fees ranging from $10,000 to $35,000 for a one-hour performance.[13] "For me, these lectures were not simply money-making gigs," West explains, "but occasions to make the world my classroom," and to make "all people my congregation."[14] Those who actually attend West's lectures are treated to oracular pronouncements like the following apercus, selected at random from his 2008 book, *Hope on a Tightrope*: *Words and Wisdom*.

- You're made in the image of God. You're a featherless, two-legged, linguistically conscious creature born between urine and feces. That's us. One day your body will be the culinary delight of terrestrial worms.... The question is: Who are you going to be in the meantime, in this time and space? You don't get out of time and space alive.[15]
- Behold, that first century Palestinian Jew was born in a funky manger. He had some funky working-class parents sometimes dealing with unemployment and underemployment. He walked on some funky and dusty roads, didn't he? He brought together 12 funky folk. He didn't go out 100 miles to the vanilla suburbs, did he? He pickled them right from around where he came from. It's so easy to forget the funk in Jesus's life because our churches can become so easily deodorized.[16]

While his audiences nod agreeably, treating his mumbo-jumbo as a discourse that somehow makes sense, what they really come to hear are the progressive insults to their country and their countrymen, which West serves up at every venue and every turn:

If you view America from the Jamestown Colony, America is a corporation before it's a country. If it's a corporation before it is a country, then white supremacy is married to capitalism. Therefore, white supremacy is something that is so deeply grounded in white greed, hatred, and fear that it constitutes the very foundation for ... [a] ... democracy called the U.S.A.[17]

At the Lannan Foundation in New Mexico where he was given an arts award in 2003, West spelled out his hatred for his country, prefacing it with a rhetorical flourish: "Who wants to interrogate the dogmas of, in Socratic fashion, white supremacy, male supremacy, economic growth by means of corporate priority, the deep dogma shot through American life?" He then went on:

American imperial expansion fascinates me. We're talking about the invasion of Iraq. It's the first time America invaded a country. Whoa! [Laughter] My God, really. Grenada, Panama, we can go right down the line. [Applause] But no, 1783, George Washington himself says that we do not want to involve ourselves with the affairs of Europe, but we do expect expansion of population and territory. You say, Mr. Washington, there's some people on that land you have in mind—[laughter]—human beings whose lives are just as valuable as yours, on intimate terms with death, with imperial expansion. The same would be true with Latino brothers and sisters, with moving borders: Mexico one day, U.S. the next. It's not mediated with argument. It's imperial expansion. Forms of death. Struggle for black freedom. Civic death. Jim Crow. Jane Crow. Lynching. I'd call it American terrorism.[18]

Others might call it gibberish. But, whatever it is, it hardly qualifies as Christian charity, despite West's repeated assertion that these words bubble up from a spiritual spring inside him: "I cannot over-state my relationship to Jesus Christ." "My foundation consists of three powerful elements: family, the Socratic spirituality of seeking truth, and the Christian spirituality of bearing witness to love and justice."[19] Etc., *ad nauseam*.

One of the instructive revelations of West's self-portrait is how much of his love is directed towards figures whose careers are iden-tified with racial and religious bigotry, and not only Jeremiah Wright. The black theologian James Cone is introduced to readers as a soul mate: "I remember going with my colleagues to a conference at Yale. It was a big-time gathering of the most celebrated theologians in the world. When I walked into that hall with my brothers—James Cone, Jim Washington and Jim Forbes—man I felt like we were the Dra-matics walking on stage at the Apollo."[20] James Cone is the well-known founder of "black theology," a racist creed built on such canonical statements as this: "Theologically, Malcolm X was not far wrong when he called the white man 'the devil'," and "What we need is the destruction of whiteness, which is the source of human misery in the world."[21]

But a race-hater like Cone is far from unusual in West's circle of estimable "brothers" and friends. As an undergraduate at Harvard, West was elected co-president of the Black Student Association, in which capacity he invited prominent speakers to campus. "At the top of my list was Imamu Amiri Baraka, a seminal man of letters, a revo-lutionary black nationalist and a mesmerizing poet. I had the high honor of introducing him."[22] At the time, Amiri Baraka, formerly known as LeRoi Jones, was already a notorious black racist and gay-basher ("Most white men are trained to be fags. For this reason it is no wonder their faces are weak and blank...") and anti-Semite ("Smile jew. Dance jew. Tell me you love me, jew. I got something for you now, though.... I got the extermination blues, jew boys"). [23]

Such rancid sentiments are absorbed and made invisible in the jive ecumenical miasma of West's "thought." What matters to him is not that Baraka is a famous bigot but that the objects of his hatred are whites rather than blacks. Brother Baraka is a comrade at war with imperial America and its "white supremacist" rulers and thus progressive, and good.

West sent his invitation to Baraka to speak at Harvard in the early Seventies. By then the Harvard community no longer had the moral intelligence to be appalled by such a guest. On the evening of his appearance, the malice-drenched Baraka returned West's favor by attacking him as "a two-bit Eurocentric wrong-headed boot-licking pseudo Marxist slave to Western thought."[24] West just stood there with the indomitable gap-toothed smile that was to become the signature of his public persona, and went on with the show.

Despite the insult—or perhaps because of it—West spent the next several decades wooing Baraka until he became a family friend. He even campaigned for Baraka's son when Baraka ran for elective office in New Jersey. By this time, despite racial attitudes that would have made any white man a social pariah, Baraka was the recipient of prestigious grants from the Rockefeller and Guggenheim foundations, had won the PEN/Faulkner Award, was a professor at Rutgers, and had been appointed Poet Laureate of New Jersey. The accolades were reflections of the same cultural breakdown that had made West's own success possible.

Eventually, Baraka was defrocked as professor and poet laureate after going a bridge too far by writing a poem called "Somebody Blew Up America," which blamed 9/11 on the Jews.[25] None of these unsavory details are mentioned in *Brother West*. Evidently, a progressive prophet, buoyed by the knowledge that the elite culture shares his prejudices, has no need to explain his adulation for a bigot who is also black.

Another unsavory visitor to Harvard during West's undergraduate years was "George X," a spokesman for the Nation of Islam and the cult of Elijah Muhammad. As West reports, "We black students were curious, eager, and excited to see what George X, the minister representing the Honorable Elijah Muhammad had to say. We packed the hall."[26] The warm reception afforded by Harvard students to the emissary of a racist cult was one more sign of the ominous cultural turn taking place. The "Honorable" Elijah Muhammad was the prophet of a religion in which white people were depicted and damned as "blue-eyed devils." According to its crackpot theology, white people were the invention of a mad scientist named Yacub who created them 6,000 years ago in an experiment gone awry. Yacub had diluted their blood causing a melanin deficiency, which made them morally defective.

In Elijah Muhammad's version of Armageddon, God was going to destroy the white devil race and bring to an end the misery they had caused.[27] One did not have to look far to see the affinities with the theology of James Cone or the rantings of Amiri Baraka. That Harvard students would seek out a spokesman with such toxic views was noteworthy in itself. Prior to the cultural upheavals of the Sixties, no such episode could have taken place in any institution of higher learning, let alone on a prestigious Ivy League campus.

On the appointed evening for George X's address, there was a dramatic confrontation: "The minister began speaking," recalls West.

> He was an articulate and intelligent man, but when he referred to Malcolm X as a "dog," I was startled. Though

Malcolm had been shot six years earlier, his murder still felt painfully close. The minister's speech went on, and then, for no apparent reason, he found it necessary to call Malcolm "dog" a second time. I was about to say something, but my friends, seeing I was agitated, restrained me. There were hefty Fruit of Islam guards, the paramilitary wing of the Nation, stationed at all the doors. I swallowed hard and let it pass. But the minister went out of his way to call Malcolm a "dog" for the third time, I couldn't take it. I jumped up and spoke my mind.

I said, "Who gives you the authority to call someone who loved black people so deeply a 'dog'? You better explain yourself."

"Young man," the minister said, seething with rage, "you best be careful. You're being highly disrespectful and impudent."[28]

When West refused to back down, George X threatened him: "Young brother, you'll be lucky to get out of this building alive. And if you do manage to slip out, you'll be gone in five days."

Rising to the melodrama, West was defiant: "Well, if that's the only response to my challenge, then I guess you're just going to have to take me out."[29]

A striking aspect of West's account of the incident is his failure to acknowledge the fact that Malcolm X was murdered by Nation of Islam assassins. The "death warrant" had been ordered by Elijah Muhammad, and was issued by his lieutenant Louis Farrakhan. Why, then, would it seem "shocking" when George X referred to Malcolm as a "dog"?

The sins that warranted Malcolm's execution were his rejection of Elijah Muhammad's racist bigotry and, worse, that he had revealed family secrets, in particular that the Honorable Minister had impregnated several teenagers, which not only broke the law but violated the puritanical codes he had set up for his cult. While certainly aware of these facts, West fails to mention any of them or explain why in view of this he would have any respect—then or now—for violent and degenerate criminals. On the contrary, writing from a vantage more than forty years distant, West still thinks that "[Malcolm] was wrong to have castigated the Honorable Elijah Muhammad in public," and then adds this aside: "And God knows, following Malcolm's lead, I had hardly been discreet in castigating George X. But when the Four Tops sang 'I Can't Help Myself,' they might as well have been talking about me."[30]

Friends rescued West from the confrontation with George X, after which he immediately went into hiding: "I went underground. I kept moving around from dorm room to dorm room, staying with various friends who had my back. I was afraid to attend class.... For as long as I was on the Nation's most wanted list, I didn't get a good night's sleep."

But this life-threatening episode seems not to have affected West's admiration for the Nation. Instead of reporting what had taken place to university administrators and protecting other students, West sought out "one of the most prominent Black Muslims on campus" to try to repair the breach. When they met, he solicited the student's views on what had happened, which led to this strange dialogue:

> From the Nation's point of view, you disrespected one of
> our ministers, just as Malcolm disrespected the Honorable

Elijah Muhammad. Do you realize what Minister Muhammad meant to Malcolm?

"I do," I said. "I've always believed that there's no Malcolm without Elijah.... But you all be calling the brother a dog, and I can never allow that. Not in public. That's a level of disrespect that's too much."[31]

Further conversation between the two led to "exploring each other's backgrounds [and] we got closer [until] empathy overwhelmed anger. By the end of the evening, the brother assured me that all was cool."[32]

That is the end of the incident, as related not by the 19-year-old Harvard student, but by the Princeton professor, now in his late fifties. *There's no Malcolm without Elijah.* True enough if one is referring to the racial demagogue that Malcolm X began as, before he turned his back on Elijah and the religion of hate, and was murdered for his apostasy. It was certainly Elijah Muhammad who taught Malcolm X to regard white people as blue-eyed devils who could not be redeemed, and also taught Malcolm to promote violence against them. This was why Malcolm attacked the civil rights movement and denounced Martin Luther King's historic march on Washington as "ridiculous," and preached the bullet over the ballot. It was why King refused to appear on the same platform with Malcolm as long as he was an adherent of Elijah's doctrines.

But Malcolm X eventually discarded the venomous prejudices that had drawn him to Elijah Muhammad. That is what caused him to come into fatal collision with the Nation and its future leader, Louis Farrakhan. What does the mature Cornel West have to say about this legacy? "Though I am a Martin Luther King Jr. kind of brother, the fiery passion for racial justice and deep love for black people found in the often misunderstood lineage from Malcolm X to Minister Louis Farrakhan will always be part of me."[33]

This is a striking confession. Who is misunderstanding the lineage from Malcolm to Farrakhan, other than Cornel West? Louis Farrakhan is the bloody-minded bigot who orchestrated Malcolm's assassination: "The die is set," his infamous *fatwa* went, "and Malcolm shall not escape, especially after such evil, foolish talk about his benefactor; such a man is worthy of death."[34] It is moral idiocy to refer to the "lineage from Malcolm X to Minister Louis Farrakhan," let alone to embrace it. It is perverse to regard the surrender to racism as reflecting a "deep love for black people" rather than a hatred for whites, and it is willful blindness not to see Malcolm's defection as an attempt to break free from a totalitarian cult, which was (and still is) destructive to the cause of racial harmony and the advancement of African-Americans. The ethical dimensions of the conflict between Malcolm and Elijah (and Farrakhan) are beyond Cornel West's comprehension, which is no small matter for someone who presents himself as a prophet of moral rectitude and a disciple of Jesus Christ, and who is accepted as such by the progressive culture at large.

West displays a similar myopia in addressing the ethical issues of communism and the role played by progressives as an auxiliary force in the atrocities Communists committed. During the Cold War, American progressives denied Communist crimes and alternately defended them. They worked through "peace" movements to cripple the military defenses of the Western democracies, and conducted propaganda campaigns to attack them.[35] The disciple of Socrates and Christ has nothing to say about this collusion of progressives with the perpetrators of the worst episode of mass murder and human oppression in history. Instead, he is co-chair of the "Democratic Socialists of America" an organization that defines its position on the left as "anti-anti-Communist"—that is, as an opponent of those who opposed communism. West is also an enthusiastic member of the academic movement to resurrect the ideas that inspired communism, burnishing the intellectual escutcheons of Stalinists such as Gyorgy Lukacs, Antonio Gramsci, Louis Althusser, Howard Zinn, and Eric Hobsbawm, who are not only his personal heroes but also heroes of large swathes of the current academic establishment. West is the author of several titles devoted to this resurrection project, including *Black Theology and Marxist Thought* and *The Ethical Dimensions of Marxist Thought*, which was his first book.

He is not only a cheerleader for serious Marxist intellectuals, but also the promoter of Marxist charlatans such as Bob Avakian, the American founder of the Revolutionary Communist Party, a Maoist grouplet. Calling himself "Chairman Bob" as an homage to his model, Avakian is the author of risible titles such *Mao Tse-Tung's Immortal Contribution* and *Radical Ruptures: Or Yes, Mao More Than Ever*—along with an autobiography, *From Ike to Mao and Beyond*. The preface to this book, written by a cult member, credits West with inspiring it: "A short time back, Cornel West, speaking to the important role Bob Avakian has played in the fight against white supremacy and in relation to the quest for a radically different world, suggested to Bob that he think about a memoir of his life so far."

When the memoir was complete, West provided this blurb: "Bob Avakian is a long distance runner in the freedom struggle against imperialism, racism and capitalism. His voice and witness are indispensable in our efforts to enhance the wretched of the earth. And his powerful story of commitment is timely."[36] Timely to be a Maoist in the year 2005!

West's emergence as a prominent public intellectual occurred in the 1990s and was premised on a cultivated image of himself as a reasonable radical. In particular, he had assumed a role as a bridge builder between blacks and Jews at a time when the overt anti-Semitism of black activists like Baraka had created a crisis between the two communities. In August 1991, an orthodox Jew named Yankel Rosenbaum was lynched in the Crown Heights neighborhood of Brooklyn during a riot featuring cries of "Death to the Jews" accompanied by an incendiary speech by the racial arsonist Al Sharpton. Sharpton was also prominent in a second incident in which he incited his followers to attack a Jewish store in Harlem and drive out the "white interloper." The store was torched and seven employees—all black and Hispanic—died in the fire.[37]

These incidents were accompanied by blatantly anti-Semitic outbursts from prominent literary and political figures in the African-American community, including Jesse Jackson, Stokely Carmichael (a.k.a. Kwame Ture), and Louis Farrakhan. Farrakhan, as usual, went the extra step: "You [Jews] are wicked deceivers of the American people," he raved on one occasion. "You have sucked their blood. You are not real Jews (who everyone knows were black). You are the synagogue of Satan, and you have wrapped your tentacles around the U.S. government, and you are deceiving and sending this nation to hell…. But if you choose to crucify me, know that Allah will crucify you."[38] It only made matters worse that in 1995 Farrakhan was able to organize a "Million Man March" on Washington, attracting to his podium prominent figures such as Martin Luther King III and Cornel West.

The legitimization of anti-Semitism as a public discourse so soon after the Holocaust was a profound shock to American Jews, who were also disheartened by the fact that such bigots could retain their prominence rather than suffering the kind of social ostracism that would have been the fate of whites who made parallel comments against blacks. West stepped into the middle of this *kulturkampf* as one of the few African-American figures willing to say that black anti-Semitism was something to be concerned about. "As to anti-Semitism the first step is to get our community to acknowledge that there is a problem," he wrote in a 1995 book, which was lauded for its ecumenical boldness.[39]

But the effort came with caveats, the first being West's view that the problem shouldn't be made too important ("You've got to acknowledge anti-Semitism, but not make it seem that you think that it is the major moral problem facing our community"[40]). The second was West's judgment that even its most virulent exponents—Farrakhan being the obvious example—should get a pass: "I wouldn't call the brother a racist...but a xenophobic spokesperson when it comes to dealing with Jewish humanity—but who in his own way loves black folk deeply, and that love is what we see first." The most succinct dissection of this attitude was made shortly afterwards by the literary editor of the liberal *New Republic*, Leon Wieseltier, who said of West, "Nothing of his own is alien to him. He finds human truths in inhuman lies."[41]

West found a partner for his new campaign in former Sixties radical Michael Lerner, who had founded the "Seattle Liberation Front," a violent "guerrilla" group, which set out to emulate the Communist Vietcong.[42] Subsequently, Lerner became a Reconstructionist rabbi, positioning himself as a leader of progressives in search of "meaning." He founded *Tikkun* magazine, presenting himself as a "pro-Israel" progressive while promoting the propaganda of Israel's Palestinian enemies, and condemning Israel's alleged "occupation" of Palestinian lands, calling on Jews "to atone for the pain we have inflicted on the Palestinian people." This was a piece of historical illiteracy on a par with West's ramblings, since Israel was created out of the ruins of the Turkish empire, which was not Arab and certainly not "Palestinian." The Arabs had waged five aggressive wars against Israel, refusing to sign peace agreements when their aggressions were repelled, which was the only reason there were any Israeli troops stationed in the West Bank and—until 2005—Gaza.[43]

As part of their campaign to build bridges between the African-American and Jewish communities, Lerner and West co-authored a book of dialogues called *Jews and Blacks: Let the Healing Begin.* Referred to in a blurb for the book by Senator Bill Bradley as "significant thinkers," West and Lerner embarked on a year-long lecture tour to address the issue.[44] "I loved the black-Christian, white-Jewish connection," writes West of the experience. "I see the Old Testament/New Testament narratives as part of a continuum…. As a Jewish brother, Jesus is confirming this concept. Hillel, a contemporary of Jesus is already on board the love train."[45]

But even the West-Lerner love train could not avoid the poisonous currents of anti-Semitism roiling their political communities. When they showed up at a black bookstore in Oakland, members of the Nation of Islam were there to reprise the incident at Harvard twenty years before. "At first the discussion went reasonably well," recalls West. "Then Michael said the words, 'Louis Farrakhan is a dog.'"[46] The visitors responded: "You're a dog." West was able to persuade the Nation members to back off, and berated Lerner: "Rabbi, I'm not sure you want to go around calling someone's spiritual leader and my dear brother a dog."[47] Despite West's warm feelings towards America's leading promoter of Jew-hatred, Lerner continued to embrace him as an ally and more: "I not only came to respect Cornel West's incredible intellect," Lerner gushed in their joint book, "but to love him."[48]

A similar incident occurred at Howard University, when Lerner again referred to West's dear brother as an anti-Semite. Someone in the audience objected and Lerner responded: "If you had read more books about the history of anti-Semitism, you wouldn't ask such an inane question." West jumped on Lerner: "That's the kind of arrogance that trumps any kind of conversation. Many black people associate that kind of arrogance with Jewish brothers and sisters who claim to be concerned about them. That's the stereotype. We're on tour trying to shatter the stereotype that, ironically, you're reinforcing here."[49]

At about this time, the liberals at the *New Republic* finally had enough. In a 5,500-word cover-feature called "The Decline of the Black Intellectual," Leon Wieseltier skewered West's overblown reputation. The article began by describing West as "a good man, an enemy of enmity," which was clearly not the case. But Wieseltier's sympathy for West's progressive politics made the rest of the testimony even more damning. "Since there is no crisis in America more urgent than the crisis of race, and since there is no intellectual in America more celebrated for his consideration of the crisis of race, I turned to West, and read his books. They are almost completely worthless.... West's work is noisy, tedious, slippery... sectarian, humorless, pedantic and self endeared."[50]

Describing West's judgment as "eccentric" (a kindness), Wieseltier provided multiple examples of typical Westian absurdities to support his case: "[West] observes that 'black America has yet to produce a great literate intellectual with the exception of Toni Morrison;' that 'Marx and Emerson herald self-realization and promote democracy;'... that 'Marxist thought becomes even more relevant after the collapse of communism in the Soviet Union and Eastern Europe than it was before;' that 'World War Two was a major setback for anti-imperialist struggles in black America;' that 'inter-subjectivity is the go-cart of individuality;'... that 'crack is the postmodern drug;' that 'the classical Marxist critique of religion is not an a priori rejection of religion;' and so on."[51]

In his autobiography West admits that Wieseltier's attack was wounding, but his response is a dismissal rather than a defense: "Socratic questioning—and challenging—is at the very heart of my being. But Wieseltier had no interest in challenging or questioning. He was intent on demonstrating that my life's work was a farce and I was a fraud. He was, in fact, not only dishonoring the tradition of honest exchange but corrupting it with ruthless character assassination."[52] Offering no response to the many concrete examples Wieseltier had provided of West's intellectual vacuity and preposterous attitudinizing, however, was itself an answer.

West was able to survive this attack because the liberal culture embraced him and his cause, and could not bring itself to acknowledge that a leading intellectual "of color" was an empty suit. Most importantly, they did not want to see their champion taken out of the culture wars. Writing in the *Village Voice*, feminist Ellen Willis conceded that West was someone who had been "lionized instead of engaged, over-praised and discreetly under-criticized," but defended him nonetheless because, "the left is a small beleaguered world these days and Cornel is a friend."[53] The notion that progressives constituted a "small beleaguered world" during the Clinton years is hard to square with their commanding presence in the media and university cultures, and their easy access to a sympathetic White House. But the desire to protect someone who had become a symbol of the progressive cause was certainly real.

Five years after the Wieseltier attack, progressives made a last notable attempt to clean up the public embarrassment that West had become. The effort led to the famous confrontation with the president of Harvard. As one of eighteen designated "University Professors" (out of a faculty of 2,000), West occupied a privileged height even at that elite institution. As a "University Professor" he was attached to no department or program, able to teach whatever he wanted, and required to report only to the president himself.[54] In October 2001, President Summers called West to his office to express concern that his professor was not meeting Harvard's academic standards.

Assuming that one can trust West's account (a dubious proposition), Summers opened with a particularly crass attempt to pander to his reputation as a faculty radical. According to West, Summers attempted to solicit help in harassing the only open conservative on the entire Harvard faculty, Harvey Mansfield.

> To break the ice, he told me I was just the man to help him undermine Professor Harvey Mansfield. In describing his desire to upset Mansfield, Summers used a language that he thought I'd find familiar.
>
> "Help me fuck him up," he said.[55]

West refused the request, telling Summers that "despite the intensity and intellectual ferocity that marked my debates with Mansfield ... I considered Mansfield my brother."[56] When this surreal moment was concluded, Summers got down to his business, complaining that West had cancelled three weeks of classes (a charge West denied) in order to work as political advisor to Senator Bill Bradley's campaign for the Democrats' presidential nomination. Summers added, "I also don't understand why in the world you would then go on to support another presidential candidate who didn't even have a remote chance of winning.... No one respects him."[57] This was a reference to Al Sharpton whose campaign West joined as a political advisor when Bradley dropped out of the race.

Summers then turned to the matter of West's scholarly work, or lack thereof, telling him he needed to "write an important book on a philosophical tradition to establish your authority and secure your place as a scholar." (In point of fact, West had published no scholarly work since his Ph.D. thesis—and even that was more a political tract than an academic study.) Summers was quite specific: West needed to produce a work that was noticed in "peer-reviewed" scholarly journals and not just in popular magazines such as *Time* and the *New York Review of Books.* Finally, Summers was distressed that his professor had spent the previous year composing a "rap" album called *Sketches of My Culture* which featured West as the rapper. Here Summers' comment was characteristically blunt: "Professor West, you have to cease making rap albums which are an embarrassment to Harvard."

It was a quixotic attempt to uphold an academic standard that had been shredded long before when West was hired to elite faculties like Harvard. But Cornel West was used to riding the waves of racial grievance to unearned success. For thirty years the race card had trumped all standards to his benefit, and he was not about to be intimidated, even by a powerful university president and former cabinet member:

> "Professor Summers, when you say 'an embarrassment to Harvard,' which Harvard are you talking about?"
>
> "The Harvard I have been hired to lead," he said.
>
> "But your Harvard, Professor Summers, is not my Harvard. And I'm as much Harvard as you are. Look, we all know that Harvard has a white supremacist legacy, a male supremacist legacy, an anti-Semitic legacy, a homophobic legacy. And we also know that Harvard has a legacy that's critical of those legacies. That's the Harvard I relate to."[58]

If the dispute had been over an affirmative action sinecure rather than the academic duties of faculty at one of the world's pre-eminent research institutions, West's argument might have had some semblance of coherence. Instead, it only exposed the subversive agendas of the tenured left, in particular its determination to make the university into a political tool for promoting its own sectarian worldview. It also revealed the lack of allegiance that faculty radicals such as West had to the institutions that employed them, and for that matter towards their country. Just as there were two Harvards for progressives like West, there were also two Americas—an America whose reality was "imperialist," "racist," and "white supremacist," with which they were at war, and an America whose "legacy" was their fantasy of a redeemed future, which was the only America to which they felt loyal.

On leaving Summers' office, West laid plans to turn his back on Harvard and accept an invitation to a post at Princeton, which had been immediately offered by the university's president. As for Harvard's own president, West had announced on leaving their meeting that Larry Summers had "a problem with black people," and further: "Larry Summers is the Ariel Sharon of American higher education." This was a barbed reference to the Prime Minister of Israel who had been thoroughly demonized by Palestinian terrorists and their sympathizers in the American left. "The man's arrogant, he's an ineffective leader," West said of Summers, "and when it comes to these sorts of delicate situations, he's a bull in the China shop."[59]

Of the two antagonists, it turned out to be West who had the superior sense of his academic audience. In short order, faculty progressives rose to his defense while Summers was immediately on his knees apologizing for his insensitivity and begging West not to leave.

But it was already too late for Summers to retrieve the situation. He had previously provoked West's progressive supporters by decrying their campaign to boycott Israel and undermine the Jewish state as it confronted enemies dedicated to its destruction. Early in his brief tenure, Summers had impoliticly condemned the divestment movement in blunt terms: "Profoundly anti-Israel views are increasingly finding support in progressive intellectual communities. Serious and thoughtful people are advocating and taking actions that are anti-Semitic in their effect...."[60] Cornel West was one of them.

While West went on to Princeton, Summers continued his progress towards becoming the first president in the history of modern research universities to be censured by his own faculty (or the 10 percent who bothered to vote), and then forced to resign. The denouement came after a second conflict, this time with Harvard feminists who were outraged when he expressed the politically incorrect idea that men might have higher aptitudes for mathematics than women (arguably a scientific fact). In the battle that ensued, ideologically driven members of the Harvard faculty were able to prevail, despite the support Summers received from a group of donors headed by David Rockefeller which withheld $400 million in pledged funds in a vain effort to save him.[61]

As in other episodes of his career, West's Harvard victory was only possible because of his role as a symbol of progressive aspirations and a purveyor of progressive clichés. These included his view of himself as a perennial racial victim, his opposition to America's role as a defender of individual freedom, his support for the enemies of the Jewish state, his indictment of American society as racist, sexist and oppressive, and his resurrection of discredited Marxist illusions about a socialist millennium. West's tireless promotion of progressive myths enlisted the support of radical faculty and cultural institutions like the *New York Times*, which swallowed hard at repeated examples of his intellectual nullity, then rallied to his cause. There is no other explanation for the ability of a shallow, vain, and vacuous intellect, a friend and defender of anti-Semites and racists, to attain the cultural prominence and receive the adulation that Cornel West has enjoyed.

In the final analysis, this saga cannot be viewed either as an isolated story or an innocent one. It could not have occurred were it not also about what has happened to the nation's culture, to the institutional standards that support its achievements and the intellectual skepticism that normally keeps it honest. It is the story of values and constraints removed to make possible a career that is morally offensive and intellectually preposterous. It is thus also a measure of the cultural decline since Cornel West was admitted to Harvard half a century ago.

The intervening years have seen progressives mount a relentless and successful assault on America's heritage and its institutional framework. The assault has been historical, indicting the builders of America as agents of bigotry and oppression, and also contemporary—condemning America's wars in defense of freedom as imperial aggressions of greed and conquest. The attacks are inspired by envy and hatred of others—white people, successful people, males, Jews, (white) Christians, and businessmen—who are held accountable for an America that progressives despise.

In this corrosive cause, Cornel West has been a prominent if also banal voice. In 2004, he published a tract called *Democracy Matters*, which sold 100,000 copies, making it to the fifth slot on the *New York Times* best-seller list, and was hailed by the *Boston Globe* as written "in the vein of Socrates." The book's subtitle described its agenda: "Winning the Fight Against Imperialism"—by which he meant the democracy that had raised him to heights he did not deserve, and crowned him with honors he had not earned.

For progressives like West, the democracy that matters is not the one we inhabit but the one Marxists promised and then discredited by piling up continents of corpses and enslaving millions in the effort to realize their impossible schemes. Of America's actual democracy, West has this to say: "The American democratic experience is unique in human history not because we are God's chosen people to lead the world or because we are always a force for good in the world, but because of our refusal to acknowledge the deeply racist and imperial roots of our democratic project."[62]

For Cornel West the great conflict of our times is the war against American oppression. "Let us not be deceived," he writes. "The great dramatic battle of the 21st Century is the dismantling of empire" and the greatest threats are "three dominating, anti-democratic dogmas."[63] The first dogma is "free market fundamentalism—just as dangerous as the religious fundamentalisms of our day." In other words, America's commitment to free markets is just as threatening as the bloodthirsty jihad of our terrorist enemies who regard us as infidels and seek to wipe America and its ally Israel from the face of the earth.[64] The second threat is "aggressive militarism," exemplified by America's war on the jihadists in Afghanistan and Iraq. "Fashioned out of the cowboy mythology of the American frontier fantasy, the dogma of aggressive militarism is a lone-ranger strategy that employs 'spare-no-enemies' tactics." In other words we are actually *worse* than the religious fanatics who have attacked us because in West's fantasy world it is we who are the predators, who lack moral restraints.

The third threat, according to West, is "escalating authoritarianism," by which he means the measures we have adopted to defend ourselves from terrorist attacks at home and abroad. "The Patriot Act is but the peak of an iceberg that has widened the scope of … repression."[65] The security measures we have taken to defend our citizens from enemies willing to murder tens of thousands of innocents constitute "the gangsterization of America."[66] In other words, in the fight for global justice, we are the criminals and therefore our citizens are fair game. The self-appointed task of prophets like West is to disarm America to make the world safe for her enemies. As in everything West writes, there is nothing original in this indictment. Its banalities are the boilerplate of the progressive faith, and its themes continue the squalid tradition of American radicalism that has consistently found in America's enemies objects of sympathy and support, while America is worthy only of its hostility and contempt.

Because West is a sentimentalist, his prose illuminates the essential form of the progressive attack. *"I wouldn't call the brother a racist … but a xenophobic spokesperson when it comes to dealing with Jewish humanity—but who in his own way loves black folk deeply, and that love is what we see first."* Support for hate in the name of love. Because America's enemies allegedly speak for the oppressed, progressives like Cornel West will love them first. In the vocabulary of the left, the "oppressed" cannot be racists and cannot be murderers and cannot threaten *us*. They are the victims, and we the devil incarnate.

Cornel West can be seen as a progressive version of the Stepin Fetchit stereotype—absurd in his stumbling efforts to impersonate an intellectual and to wear the mantle of a prophet of social change. But he is also the archetype of an American radicalism that has set out to destroy the American experiment, whose strength can be measured in his unmerited triumphs and ridiculous career.

CHAPTER FOUR

Pardoned Bombers

It was the usual things of life that filled her with silent rage,
which was natural enough, inasmuch as to her vision
almost everything that was usual was iniquitous.... The
most secret, the most sacred hope of her nature
was that she might some day ... be a martyr
and die for something.

—Henry James, *The Bostonians*

During the days of summer, Santa Monica's Third Street Promenade bustles with strollers who come to take in the antics of street artists and mimes. The scene recalls the Renaissance Faires, which I used to visit as a young radical in Berkeley in the 1960s. On a balmy August evening, barely a month before Islamic jihadists struck the World Trade Center, my wife and I had joined these crowds when we came on one of Bill Clinton's presidential pardons, a radical bomber who was now out of prison and back on the streets.

The last time I had seen Linda Evans was in Berkeley, thirty-two years before. She had come to the University of California campus with another revolutionary named Ted Gold to speak to a packed hall of students. Evans and Gold were leaders of a radical sect called "Weatherman," which had taken over the protest organization SDS and, in an act of revolutionary bravado, shut it down for good. It was, they said, a case of "trashing the pig." Radical as SDS was, it wasn't radical enough for the Weathermen. Evans and Gold were in Berkeley to recruit troops for a global race war they and their comrades were certain had already begun and which they intended to join. They wanted to "bring the war home."

The evening's harangues were striking in the contempt they displayed for the hundreds of students who had come to hear them and whom they regarded as hypocrites and cowards because they had not already joined the conflict. In the global "race war," the only morally defensible position for whites was to form a fifth column of saboteurs inside the "belly of the beast" and provide support for the darker races in revolt. It was our moral duty to blow things up. "Vietnam is burning," Evans screamed; "it's only white skin privilege that prevents American cities from being torched as they deserve." Everyone in the room understood that this meant Berkeley. Only our "white skin privilege"—our racism—prevented us from lighting the match.

A few months after issuing this summons, Evans and Gold disappeared into the "Weather Underground"—the clandestine organization led by Bill Ayers and Bernardine Dohrn—which the Weathermen had created to carry on the war behind enemy lines. "War communiqués" issued by Dohrn contained a formal declaration of hostilities against "Amerikkka." A series of symbolic bombings followed—the Capitol Building in Washington, police stations in San Francisco and Los Angeles, and the Pentagon. Then, on March 6, 1970, three Weather soldiers accidentally blew themselves up in a Greenwich Village townhouse where they were making a bomb filled with roofing nails. They had intended to detonate their anti-personnel device at a dance for draftees and their dates at nearby Fort Dix. Ted Gold was one of the three dead bomb builders, identified by a finger that was found in the rubble.

Months later Linda Evans was arrested in Detroit for transporting weapons and explosives, and for crossing state lines to incite a riot, a charge related to the Days of Rage the Weathermen had conducted when they were still above ground. With the help of a team of leftwing attorneys, Evans was able to get the charges thrown out because the wiretaps that identified her had been unauthorized. On her release she resumed the war as a self-described fighter against "racism/white supremacy and Zionism," and later a supporter of the Communist guerrilla armies in Central America. A "political prisoners" website characterizes her activities over the next fifteen years as "working to develop clandestine resistance, capable of conducting armed struggle as part of a multi-level overall revolutionary strategy."[1]

Evans was arrested again on May 11, 1985. This time she was convicted of acquiring weapons and fake IDs, organizing safe houses, and conducting terrorist actions. Her targets included the U.S. Capitol Building, the National War College, the Navy Yard Computer Center, the Navy Yard Officers Club, Israeli Aircraft Industries, the FBI, and the New York Patrolman's Benevolent Association. When police apprehended her, she was in possession of 740 pounds of dynamite. She was sentenced to forty years in prison.[2]

Thanks to support from the progressive left, however, she was to be released again. One year before the World Trade Center attack, Evans' supporters persuaded Congressman Jerrold Nadler of New York to petition the White House for a presidential pardon. Nadler was a leftwing member of the House Judiciary Committee, which had oversight of the nation's security measures. After 9/11 he became one of the most ferocious opponents of the security programs that were put in place by the Bush administration to thwart further attacks. Nadler's appeal to Clinton was successful. As the last hours of his presidency expired, he signed a pardon for Evans, who still had twenty-four years remaining on her sentence. Free and unrepentant, she resumed her revolutionary activities, which included a recruitment session in the Midnight Special bookstore.

It was a habit of mine, whenever I was in the vicinity of the Santa Monica promenade, to stop by the bookstore, which was a gathering place for radicals, to look over their latest literature and see what the comrades were up to. On this occasion, I noticed a display in the window announcing that the famous radical Linda Evans would be presenting a film that evening and giving a talk about "political prisoners." When my wife and I entered the store, I saw a darkened space behind a row of bookshelves, and we went over to where a cluster of about thirty people were seated on folding chairs to watch the film.

The showing was almost over by the time we sat ourselves down, but we were able to catch a final sequence about Laura Whitehorn, a member of the Weather Underground and other violent radical groups, who had just been released on parole. As the film concluded, a scroll appeared on the screen with a long list of "political prisoners" who were still in jail. As the lights went up, Evans emerged from the group and asked the audience to circle its chairs around her. I had remembered her as a small, fiery, woman, with blond hair and a pretty but flinty face flushed with revolutionary fervor. The face and demeanor were softer now, and freshly washed with tears from watching her comrades in the film, although she had undoubtedly seen it many, many times.

She wiped her eyes and apologized for the emotional display. I noticed that the years had piled flesh on her small frame giving her a roly-poly look and making her seem softer still. In place of the steely voice, there was now a mothering hush, whose subdued tones were well suited to the role she had contrived for the evening as the leader of a support group for political victims who had been forgotten by everyone else. She began by noticing that even as we sat there people were being "oppressed" in America by white racism and imperialism.

I found myself wondering how her audience reconciled this grim picture with the carnival of Saturday night revelers on the promenade outside. Oblivious of the cognitive dissonance, Evans pressed on with her tales of social woe, now focusing on a comrade still in prison who was unable to attend her pottery classes because of "the arthritis in her hands," as if her affliction was yet another injustice administered by the country with whom she was obviously still at war. Passing from the subject of her arthritic friend to the real business of the evening, Evans devoted the next twenty minutes to the ongoing persecutions of three individuals—Sara Jane Olson, Jamil Abdullah Al-Amin, and Kathy Boudin—who were coming up for trial or parole hearings and needed public support. Their stories, if she had told them accurately, would have provided a mini-history of the dark end of the Sixties left. Instead, Evans restricted her accounts to aspects of their cases that could be shaped to fit a narrative of suffering at the hands of an enemy that was invariably racist and white.

Since this narrative necessarily contained unusual gaps, it was not surprising when the first question asked was what her subjects had done to put themselves in the situations they were in. At first she seemed taken aback, as though the answer had already been provided in her talk. Obviously, those who were oppressed could not be held accountable for their suffering. But she gathered herself and began a response, focusing first on Sara Jane Olson and then on Jamil Al-Amin, both of whom had trials scheduled for the fall.

Olson's real name was Kathy Soliah, and she had been a member of the Symbionese Liberation Army, a gang of violent radicals who made headlines when they kidnapped the heiress Patty Hearst and offered to ransom her in exchange for millions of dollars in food for the homeless. This was new background information that Evans carefully sifted of unruly details even as she shared it. Soliah, she said, had not been a member of the organization when they conducted the kidnapping, which was true. But Soliah had also publicly praised their violent acts and joined the group soon after. In Evans' account, Soliah was accused of attempting to "fire bomb" a police car. I noticed that she hesitated over the words "fire" and "bomb" as though despite all her years of revolutionary dedication, she was still sensitive to the fact that others might find such activities problematic. In fact, even this "information" fell far short of the truth. Soliah was not accused of attempting to fire bomb a police car. She was accused of placing *pipe bombs* under two police cars, intending to detonate them and kill the occupants, who were targeted solely because they were officers of the law. The men were spared only because the bombs malfunctioned. "It didn't even go off," Evans whined, as though the failure to succeed at a murder exculpated the perpetrator.

Eventually, the main individuals involved in the SLA were killed in a shootout with police and the radical episode came to an end. Soliah decided to return to her previous life, changing her name to Sara Jane Olson, marrying a doctor in Minnesota, and raising three children, while continuing her political wars as a member of the progressive left. Evans seized on this story line to underscore Soliah's "innocence" and to condemn a justice system that had indicted its victim for alleged crimes committed long ago by an organization she had left. Soliah/Olson's attorney, Shawn Chapman, was sitting among us and rose to second these observations.

In defending their comrade, neither Chapman nor Evans ever got around to explaining what the Symbionese Liberation Army had actually done, aside from the kidnapping of a rich heiress, to merit such retribution from the law. Before kidnapping Hearst they had assassinated the first black superintendent of Oakland's public schools, executing him with cyanide-tipped bullets. His offense had been to approve a program that issued ID cards to high school students in an effort to keep drug dealers off school property. In the course of a subsequent action, they had also killed a pregnant customer at a bank they were robbing. Soliah took part in this robbery, along with setting the pipe bombs as an SLA soldier.[3]

Evans next turned to the case of Jamil Abdullah Al-Amin, who had achieved an hour of fame in the Sixties as H. Rap Brown, proclaiming "violence is as American as cherry pie" and inciting blacks to "burn America down."[4] Subsequently Brown was sent to prison for robbery. There he converted to Islam and changed his name. He was paroled in 1976 and moved to Atlanta where he founded the Atlanta Community Mosque. He also became a community organizer and soon emerged as a national figure in the Islamic community, being elected in 1990 as vice president of the American Muslim Council.

These activities came to a halt when he was arrested for the ambush-murder of a policeman in 1995. Evans omitted the charge in her account of Al-Amin, presenting him as a pious "Imam" at a Muslim temple, and a community worker who helped the drug-addicted and the poor, and who for this reason had been targeted by police. "There was a shootout," she said, in her summary of the events that led to his arrest. Two police officers had gone to Al-Amin's home at night with a warrant for traffic tickets. "Who arrests people at night for traffic tickets?" Evans asked.

In fact, Al-Amin had been previously charged with possessing a stolen car, driving without insurance, and impersonating a police offer. He had failed to show up for his court date and that was the reason the officers were delivering a warrant for his arrest when they were ambushed and one of them was killed. Continuing her account, Evans remarked that the officer who survived the "shoot-out" had reported that the fleeing gunman was wounded and bleeding. But when police tracked Al-Amin three days later to another state, Evans claimed he had no wound. In her telling this was confirmation that it was a clear case of racist police targeting a member of an oppressed community because of his community activism.

In fact, both police officers were black (another detail Evans omitted). They had been ambushed with a firearm registered to Al-Amin, which was found in his possession when he was captured. Evans did not attempt to explain why an innocent man would flee and hide out for three days until a massive manhunt tracked him down, or why Atlanta's police force, whose chief was also black, would target and then falsely imprison a well-known civil rights activist who had become a holy man serving the poor. Or why Atlanta's black mayor and black community would support the prosecution of Jamil Al-Amin.

At the conclusion of Evans' story, an elderly gentleman in a straw hat sitting near me asked her how she defined the term "political prisoner," which she had applied to all her subjects. "Every prisoner in American jails is a victim of political circumstance," she replied. The idea that all criminals are political rebels is a long-standing trope of the political left, and the argument of texts by academic Communists like Eric Hobsbawm and Angela Davis, as well as the premise of an entire radical movement to abolish "the prison-industrial complex." These radicals view crime not as an activity of anti-social individuals, that is, as an expression of character, but as a product of "political circumstance." Because radicals are engaged in a war with established order—with morality and law—they regard violators of that order as social victims and potential political allies. Absorbed in a narcissism that will justify any means necessary to change the social order, they are oblivious to the damages their own crimes inflict.

The separate reality inhabited by radicals was brought home in a *New York Times* story I read shortly after my evening at the Midnight Special bookstore. It was about the third "political prisoner" whom Linda Evans chose to feature in her appeal—the Weather Underground terrorist Kathy Boudin. Boudin had been a member of the same close-knit network that included Evans and Whitehorn, and was coming up for an appeal hearing before her parole board. The *Times* was running a series of articles designed to make Boudin's case as sympathetic as possible to its readers in order to help secure her release.

Kathy Boudin was the daughter of a prominent and well-to-do family. Her father, Leonard, was a famous leftwing lawyer, who represented Fidel Castro and other Communists and radicals whose agendas he supported, but was invariably described in papers like the *Times* as a "prominent civil rights attorney." Kathy had gone to expensive private schools, and graduated magna cum laude from Bryn Mawr. In the 1970s, when the Weather Underground imploded amidst mutual recriminations, she joined the May 19 Communist Organization and became associated with a violent gang called the Black Liberation Army. The BLA conducted a series of bank robberies allegedly aimed at financing "the revolution." Their crimes included a $1.6 million heist of a Brinks armored car, during which two officers and a security guard were killed in cold blood. Boudin was part of a getaway team for the robbery. She was arrested at a roadblock, tried and convicted, and sentenced to life in prison.

At her parole hearing, Boudin presented herself as a changed woman, a claim powerfully bolstered by the *Times* series. "Today," the *Times* reported, "her supporters say Ms. Boudin is a different woman. During her 20 years in prison she has helped to create several innovative programs for AIDS victims, incarcerated mothers and inmates seeking to take college courses."[5] But she never repudiated her radical past. The *Times* overlooked it, but Boudin remained a committed radical, allowing her infant Chesa to be adopted by two of her unrepentant accomplices, Bill Ayers and Bernardine Dohrn. Chesa has grown up to become a well-known leftist in his own right, dedicated—in his own words—to carrying on his parents' "fight against U.S. imperialism around the world."[6] If Boudin were truly a changed woman, she would have turned her back on her criminal associates and come clean about her crimes and the ideas that led to them. But then she would also have deprived herself of the support groups lobbying for her release.

While the *Times* presented her as a sympathetic figure and lent credibility to her claims of remorse, Boudin showed no more concern for the surviving members of her victims' families than she had for the victims themselves. The liberal writer Susan Braudy, while researching a book on the Boudin family, visited Kathy in prison after attending a memorial service for the slain officers. She mentioned to Boudin that among those present at the service was the son of Waverly Brown who had been eighteen at the time of his father's murder. "Who?" said Boudin. "I never knew the guy had a son."[7] Braudy was taken aback. "Kathy wrote poignant poems about her incarceration. She lectured other prisoners about making amends to crime victims, but in the 20 years since the Brinks robbery she had not learned that Waverly Brown, the young black policeman slain by the BLA in Nyack moments after she'd convinced him to put away a gun, had had a teenage son."[8]

As part of its effort to promote Boudin's release, the *Times* ran yet another 3,000-word feature, this time about her graduation from the college program she had created in prison. The program was funded by leftwing supporters such as the actress Glenn Close and *Vagina Monologues* author Eve Ensler. Boudin's boosters also included the *Nation* magazine, numerous organizations advocating "prisoner rights" and "social justice," and a cohort of socially prominent representatives of New York's cultural elite.

The Black Liberation Army was not Boudin's first introduction to criminal violence. She had been a leader of the Weather Underground and was a survivor of the team constructing the anti-personnel bomb, which had prematurely exploded, killing Ted Gold and two of their comrades. Unchastened by the tragedy, Boudin continued her terrorist career, participating in at least twelve known subsequent bombings. When the Underground dissolved into warring factions in the mid-Seventies, Boudin and several of her comrades, including Laura Whitehorn, joined the May 19 Communist Organization. The group then formed a working alliance with the Black Liberation Army, referring to their alliance as "The Family."

The botched attempt to rob the Brinks armored car left nine children, ranging in age from two months to twenty-one years, without fathers, and with permanent wounds beyond the powers of the courts to heal.[9] Waverly Brown had been the first black policeman hired to the Nyack police force as the result of a lengthy civil rights struggle undertaken by blacks and whites in the Nyack community. This is how Kathy Boudin explained her role in the robbery to the *New York Times* twenty years later: "I went out that day with a lot of denial. I didn't think anything would happen; in my mind, I was going back to pick up my child at the baby-sitter's."

Boudin was a trained member of the gang's getaway team. She had rented a U-Haul to serve as one of the vehicles in the escape plan. Its driver, David Gilbert, was the father of the child she had left with the sitter. They had parked the U-Haul a few miles from the robbery, where they planned to wait for the six perpetrators—all members of the Black Liberation Army—and provide them with a change of vehicles. On cue, the six climbed into the back compartment of the U-Haul with the stolen money and automatic weapons in hand. The U-Haul drove off but was stopped moments later at a roadblock set up by police who had been told to intercept a van occupied by African-American males.

When officers Waverly Brown and Peter O'Grady approached the Boudin van, they were momentarily confused by the sight of a middle-class white woman fleeing from the vehicle. Boudin took advantage of the unthreatening impression she made, shouting, "Put the gun back." When she repeated the plea, O'Grady and Brown dropped their guard and holstered their weapons as they went to inspect the rear of the vehicle. Its doors then suddenly burst open, and Boudin's accomplices began firing multiple rounds at the two officers who had no chance of defending themselves.[10]

Susan Rosenberg was a revolutionary colleague of both Evans and Boudin, an accomplice in the Brinks robbery, and also a Clinton pardon. Like Boudin, Rosenberg had attended fancy private institutions such as the Walden School and Barnard College. After the Weather Underground dissolved, she too joined the "The Family" to work with the Black Liberation Army. The BLA was in fact a small gang of black criminals and drug addicts, who had adopted a political veneer while conducting a string of armed robberies and murders in the New York-New Jersey area. They justified these activities as "funding the revolution," but used the money they stole to buy a mansion and feed their addictions. The middle class white radicals, whom they recruited to help them, rented and drove the vehicles that facilitated their escapes.[11] The bond that united them was the idea that together they were going to change America and the world.

"May 19th"—the date the white radicals chose for their organizational name—symbolized this bond. May 19 was the birthday of Ho Chi Minh and Malcolm X. It was also the day that the Black Liberation Army had targeted and murdered a black and white police team in Harlem to punish them for their service to the enemy and for working together. The white officer was machine-gunned execution-style while pleading for his life.

As members of The Family, Rosenberg and Boudin also provided logistical support for the prison escape of Black Liberation Army leader and convicted cop-killer Joanne Chesimard, a.k.a. Assata Shakur, who then fled to Communist Cuba. Both women wrote adoring poems to Shakur, who had been serving a life sentence for one of the more than half a dozen known murders she and her cohorts had committed.

Rosenberg was finally captured in 1984 at a New Jersey warehouse where she and Linda Evans were unloading explosives they planned to detonate at various government offices. Also in their possession were fourteen weapons, including an Uzi submachine gun. On her arrest Rosenberg immediately became a progressive hero, supported by celebrity defenders of political criminals like Noam Chomsky and William Kunstler, both of whom actively lobbied for her release. Since she had been sentenced to fifty-eight years for her crimes, her prosecutor, Rudy Giuliani, decided not to pursue charges in connection with the killing of the three officers in Nyack. Sixteen years later,

Rosenberg and Evans won the support of Congressman Jerrold Nadler and were pardoned by President Clinton on his last day in office.

Because the left is inspired by the fantasy of a future that can never be realized, it is never defeated by its defeats. Evans, Rosenberg, and Boudin are still part of an ongoing community of political radicals, some still serving prison terms, while others form networks of support for "political prisoners." By concealing their agendas behind an aura of idealism and victimhood, they are able to manipulate others into supporting them as "prisoners of conscience." But despite efforts like that of the *Times* to burnish their image, these are not prisoners of conscience. On the contrary, they are prisoners without conscience, incapable of even a minimal accounting for what they did fifteen or thirty years ago, or what—in the right circumstances—they would willingly do in the future.

Two years after my encounter at the Midnight Special bookstore, Kathy Boudin was paroled, having served twenty-two years of her life sentence. Her release was secured at the second of her parole hearings, during which she repeated her previous performance, first by lying about her role in the robbery and then about her foreknowledge of the crime. She claimed to be only "a passenger" in the getaway car and unaware of the intentions of her armed comrades. She claimed never to have been "directly involved in violence" in her life, although she had spent most of her adult years in two outlaw gangs dedicated to violence and war, and had been the member of a cell that constructed an anti-personnel bomb designed to kill 18-year-old draftees attending a dance at Fort Dix.[12]

She was granted her parole and set free by two African-American parole board commissioners who were sympathetic to her plea. They accepted her claim that she had committed her crimes because she felt guilty for being white. One of the commissioners, Daizzee Bouey, asked Boudin if her involvement in the crime was because "she felt she had not done anything to validate her commitment to civil rights." Boudin replied, "Yes, I think that's right."[13] But like her other excuses, this too was a lie. Boudin had been a civil rights activist in her teens, and in her twenties had worked to help African-Americans in poor communities in Newark and Cleveland until she became bored with the lack of attention her efforts were receiving and proceeded to her headline-grabbing exploits as an "underground" terrorist, and then as a getaway driver for a revolutionary gang.[14] Virtually all of her violent crimes, moreover, were committed five, ten, and fifteen years after the passage of the Civil Rights Acts, and after she decided that the civil rights movement, which was non-violent, was too tame.

Eight years after Boudin's release, I received an email about Boudin's accomplice, Susan Rosenberg. The sender was a progressive woman, whom I will call Rachel, and who was the head of a large charity organization that provided humanitarian services that were non-political in nature. Despite our political differences, she had befriended my late daughter and had done me a personal favor, and was now asking for one in return:

February 26, 2011 9:47:45 AM PST

Dear David,

    You may or may not know that Susan Rosenberg, a woman you once attacked because of her past political activity, has worked at [my organization][15] for the past decade, moving up from a part time position in our education department where she worked initially on AIDS education programs similar to those she had designed and implemented when she was in prison. For the last five years she has been the extraordinarily able director of our entire communications department, helping to design and develop our website and prepare our publications for volunteers, donors and prospective supporters. She does an unbelievably effective job for us.

Susan has written a book about her experiences as an activist and about her time in American prisons. The book puts her activities into the context in which she now can understand, analyze and critique them. It also describes quite graphically the often horrendous experiences she had in and with the prison system.

David, I have no idea if you have the time or inclination to read the book, although I think that you, like me, would learn something from it. That is up to you. What I am beseeching you to do is to act as you wish others had acted toward you and not to launch an attack on the book or on Susan as the book comes to public light and she embarks [on leave from us] on a book tour that is, of course, very important to her and important to getting her message out.

Rachel

I answered her within the hour:

February 26, 2011 10:43:08 AM PST

Dear Rachel,

There is not a lot I wouldn't do for you and I will do my best in this case and will certainly give Susan Rosenberg's book a fair read. I have always encouraged second thoughts on the part of radicals and highlighted them when they have occurred. I do not expect everyone to agree with me and have a long record of praising progressives when they do good things, you among them. That said, the title of her book—*An American Radical: How I Was a Political Prisoner in My Own Country*—is not promising. How was a woman who participated in an armed robbery that left 9 children fatherless a "political prisoner in my own country?"[16] However, I will promise you this: I am never going to attack [your organization] whether through Susan or anyone else if that was your concern. As for Susan herself, insofar as she is honest about what she did, cognizant of crimes she committed and candid about positions she once took that she now regrets—I will acknowledge and praise her for that in any public comments I happen to make.

David

I then sat down to read the book. When I finished it, I wrote to Rachel again.

April 5, 2011 12:35:12 PM PDT

Dear Rachel,

I have now read Susan Rosenberg's book *An American Radical*. If I decide to write about it eventually, I will do so well after her promotional window has closed and after her book tour has ended, as you requested.

That said, I feel I owe you a more detailed response to your comments about the book itself, in particular that the author has had second thoughts about her past activities and that I could learn something from her experience. I disagree with you on both counts and will explain to you why.

Rosenberg's book is not an account of the author's life and therefore not really a reflection on what she did before going to jail. Consequently, it offers no serious reappraisals of how she got there. In her view, her arrest was an injustice—not because she was innocent of the crimes she was accused of committing, but because in her eyes the crimes were not crimes when looked at from a revolutionary perspective. Hence the subtitle of her book, "A Political Prisoner in My Own Country." In her view she was jailed for her political ideas.

An American Radical is almost entirely an account of her time in prison. It is intended as an indictment of the prison system and the authorities who put her there and managed her stay. It is, in essence, a continuation of the political indictment of American society and the American political system as racist and oppressive that led her to commit the crimes for which she was jailed.

In my eyes, these views of American society, which she still holds, are more extreme—not to say bizarre—in today's context, with Barack Obama in the White House, than they were when she was a leader of the May 19 Communist Organization and a working partner with the Black Liberation Army more than thirty years ago. More importantly, there is not a sentence in her book where Rosenberg considers or attempts to come to terms with the irreparable damage she and her comrades inflicted on the lives of the nine children of the three officers they killed, their parents, or their loved ones. Nor is there any remorse for the families of the five officers killed by her comrades in the Black Liberation Army.

Rosenberg says she thought about the officers in the Brinks robbery—but never tells us those thoughts and never takes personal responsibility for the deaths, which she regards as one would casualties in a war rather than victims of a crime. All of Rosenberg's concerns in this book are about herself and what she still perceives to be the unjust punishment of the violent radicals she chose to make her comrades, who did commit violent criminal acts against innocent people.

One of the officers she and her group killed was Waverly Brown, the first African-American hired to the Nyack police force, after a long struggle by civil rights activists. She has no comment on this irony. She has no second thoughts about the lives she helped to take. The only regret she actually expresses is that she "incorrectly [read] the mood of the country"—in other words that the American people were not ready for armed revolution in the years she and the Black Liberation Army were attempting to launch one by robbing banks and armored cars.

Those years by the way were years when Jimmy Carter was president and U.S. troops had been out of Vietnam for more than seven years, although she characteristically uses the Vietnam War as an excuse for her inexcusable behavior. Even more disturbing, there is not the slightest indication that thirty-odd years later she has changed her mind about what she calls the need for a "black revolution" to "end the endemic white supremacy" of the American people, even

after 63 million of them—most of them white—elected
an African-American with deep roots in the radical movement to be their president.

The author has also not changed her views about the
righteousness of being one of the leaders of a criminal
gang that murdered three officers, two when they opened
the back of the truck she and Kathy Boudin were in and
were gunned down by her armed cohorts who were inside.
Instead, she refers (falsely) to the officers as having been
killed in a "shootout"—in other words, victims of war
rather than of the criminals who killed them.

As to thinking differently about the past, here is all that
I could find: After many years in jail, Rosenberg does finally
realize that there is not going to be an armed revolution in
America any time soon, and that her efforts to start one
have failed. This leads her to reconsider her continuing
involvement in a revolutionary grouplet in prison with the
self-imposed military discipline this requires, and perhaps
to end some formal association with the group (she cannot
even bring herself to be candid about this—so it is left
frustratingly vague). At the same time she remains spiritu-
ally connected to all the violent comrades with whom she
worked and associated. There is no reason offered by her
for becoming a law-abiding citizen other than that she
thinks that armed struggle is for the moment futile.

Throughout her book Rosenberg perpetuates the
heroic myths that surround the criminals she associated
with, and similar myths about other violent revolutionaries like Mao and Che Guevara. These myths have a common thread—they absolve the revolutionary perpetrators

from responsibility for their victims. In perpetuating these myths Rosenberg creates a fertile ground for the future crimes that younger people influenced by them may commit. Towards the end of her memoir she is teaching African-Americans in prison about Robert Williams and his book *Negroes With Guns* and Eldridge Cleaver and his book *Soul On Ice*, as though these violent and marginal extremists were central figures in the struggles for dignity and equal rights for African-Americans. I think Martin Luther King would have had something to say about that.

Ultimately her adjustment to some semblance of law-abiding reality is driven by a calculus that is entirely self-centered. In misreading the possibilities for successful armed struggle, she had caused herself to be buried alive and to no real purpose. This self-pity and sense of futility is what causes the very modest change in her outlook—not any reckoning of the damage she and her comrades caused or any recognition of the benefits conferred on all people living in a capitalist democracy, even if they fall short of her expectations. The remarkable advance of African-Americans in our society in the last sixty years goes unnoticed by a woman who constantly invokes their suffering as a justification for her crimes.

An American Radical is, finally, a profoundly dishonest book, which is also why there is so little to be learned from it. Here is a characteristic passage: "On August 7, 1970, George Jackson's younger brother Jonathan entered a courtroom armed with the demand that the Soledad Brothers be released. Jonathan was killed as he drove away from the courthouse." These sentences capture the essential theme of her book: Innocent people like Jonathan Jackson are gunned down in America for demanding their rights.

As it happens, I also thought of myself as a "revolutionary" at that time, and actually took my children to Jonathan Jackson's funeral. But, deluded as I was, I would never have attempted to deceive people about the basic facts of what happened on that day. On the contrary, as a revolutionary I believed it was important to stay in touch with reality, not to deny or conceal it. I felt it was the particular responsibility of people who wanted to change the world to understand the consequences of their actions and minimize the damage they might do. Telling the truth so that others may learn from one's experience is crucial to this, which is one reason I am no longer a radical, and why Rosenberg's dishonesty is what I found most disturbing about her book.

Jonathan Jackson did not enter the Marin County courthouse "armed with [a] demand." He entered it armed with an arsenal of weapons that Angela Davis had bought for him, took three hostages (including a judge to whose chin he taped one of the gun barrels) and left the courthouse with the intention of hijacking a plane to Cuba and trading the hostages for his incarcerated brother. A year later his brother slit the throats of three guards during an escape attempt. He was not "assassinated" as Rosenberg falsely claims in her next sentence.

Nor was Jonathan Jackson "killed as he drove away from the courthouse." The police set up a roadblock to stop the kidnapping, and when he and his cohorts got out of their car and opened fire, Jonathan, the judge, and several others were killed or wounded in the gun battle that ensued. Responsibility for those deaths is on Jonathan Jackson's head, not the officers whom Rosenberg seeks to blame.

After reading Rosenberg's false accounts of these and other easily verifiable events, I think it would be reasonable to conclude that nothing she says in this book can be trusted to be the truth, particularly when she is describing the actions of those she disagrees with and regards as enemies of the people.

Rosenberg was arrested with 740 pounds of TNT in her possession and a list of targets against which she and her cohorts intended to use them. The police were looking for her because she had participated in the successful escape from prison of a convicted murderer and close associate, Assata Shakur. Shakur was the leader of the Black Liberation Army, and had been incarcerated for killing a New Jersey state trooper. In describing Shakur, Rosenberg as usual whitewashes her criminal career and excuses her criminal acts by first describing her as "a lifelong activist and continuous target of the U.S. government" and then by saying that Shakur was "ambushed" by the two highway patrol officers.

In fact, Shakur and a cohort were stopped for a broken taillight and exceeding the speed limit. Instead of cooperating with the officers, Shakur shot one of them, while her companion shot and wounded the other, then executed him with two shots to the head from his own service revolver. The officer left a wife and a 3-year-old son. This murder was standard operating procedure for Shakur and the Black Liberation Army, which had robbed a series of banks, killed four policemen and attempted to blow up a New York judge. Yet this is a person whom Rosenberg regarded—and still regards—as a comrade and a revolutionary hero.

Like her account of Shakur's arrest, Rosenberg's description of her life in prison and what she regards as her harsh treatment by prison guards reflects her continuing sense of victimhood and ongoing disconnect from reality. In her telling, the guards are racists who give her a hard time because she opposes white supremacy and is a political radical seeking social justice. A more plausible explanation is that they viewed her as a felon who had aided the escape of a cop-killer and was a direct participant in a robbery, which led to the deaths of three fellow officers. Reason enough to be angry with her and treat her harshly regardless of her political views.

Rosenberg is outraged by the long prison sentence she received for possessing 740 pounds of TNT with the intent to use it. She views this, as usual, as punishment for her leftwing views. But there were an awful lot of us who publicly expressed our leftwing—and even "revolutionary"—views without committing criminal acts or going to jail, let alone earning a 58-year sentence. It is not as though the judge imposing her sentence was unaware of her other activities and the dangers they posed to innocent people (something she remains in denial about to this day). In fact, had she not already been sentenced to this long term, her prosecutor, Rudy Giuliani, made clear that he would have tried her for her role in the Brinks robbery, which would have resulted in a life sentence. But for Rosenberg to concede this would deprive her of another opportunity to indict her government as oppressive, racist, and unjust.

There were many leftists active in the years Rosenberg chose to join a gang of violent criminals who would regard her actions as repellent, and her dishonesty and lack of contrition appalling. I am one of them. On the basis of the views expressed in this book, I have no regrets about having opposed Rosenberg's appointment as a teacher to young people. That is not because I am opposed to teachers with leftwing ideas. Phil Klinkner is a professor at the same college to which she was once appointed a visiting professor. Klinkner is a *Nation* leftist, but he is also a decent, law-abiding, and honest person whom I have publicly praised for his integrity and scholarship, despite my disagreement with his political views.

And there are others. David Weir, who is on the editorial board of the *Nation*, and Kate Coleman, a veteran writer of the left, have helped bring the facts about the murder of Betty Van Patter by the Black Panther Party to light and thus to instill a healthy caution among young people when approaching groups supporting armed revolution in a democratic society. I would feel a lot better if there were more like them.

David

I never received a reply to my letter. Nor did I expect one. I knew the reality Rachel inhabited was just as separate from mine as was that of Susan Rosenberg herself. Even though she never allowed her views to move her to criminal extremes, she shared enough of Rosenberg's fantasy of a redemptive future—a world of "social justice"—to excuse the crimes she committed as "mistakes" in the service of a noble ideal, or at least to give credence to Rosenberg's paranoid version of the facts, in which her friends and not their targets were the victims. Radicals like Rosenberg and Boudin first deceive themselves about the world they live in, and then deceive others about the actions they undertake to change it. In this way an entire community of supporters, many of whom would never break a law, will overlook the terrible crimes they committed, and the lives they changed forever and for the worse.

Both Rosenberg and Boudin were adopted, for example, by P.E.N., an association of writers that is the oldest human rights organization in the world. P.E.N.'s board included cultural luminaries like Susan Sontag and Salman Rushdie, and one of its primary missions was to defend writers imprisoned and persecuted for their ideas. Although devoid of literary credentials, Rosenberg received four P.E.N. writing awards in prison, while Boudin was awarded First Prize in P.E.N.'s 1997 contest for the best writer in prison. Rosenberg was a featured speaker at the P.E.N. "World Voices Festival" three years in a row, including the one in which she was promoting her newly published book about being a "political prisoner" in America.[17] The left-sympathetic media formed a support group as well. Rosenberg's successful pardon was preceded by a prime-time segment on the celebrated CBS show *60 Minutes*, which presented her story from her point of view. Kathy Boudin's parole appeal was supported by a sympathetic profile in the the *New Yorker*, as well as the series in the *New York Times* highlighting her "idealism" and faux reformation.

In January 2012, the *Times* devoted the cover of its Sunday magazine and a 3,000-word, four-color spread to an effort to secure the release of yet a third participant in the Brinks robbery and murders, and comrade of Rosenberg and Boudin. This time the subject was Judith Clark, another member of The Family's getaway team who had achieved notoriety during her closing statement at the trial when she declared: "Revolutionary violence is necessary, and it is a liberating force." It was a far more honest statement of what she believed at the time than anything she now said to the *Times*, or that its reporter, who was a high school friend, wrote about her current views. The story was titled "Judith Clark's Radical Transformation," and its headline falsely claimed that she had "done as much as anybody could to rehabilitate herself during her three decades in prison."[18] In the body of the story not a shred of evidence was presented to show that Clark was prepared to tell the truth about the radical networks she participated in, which included a seven-year tour of duty in the Weather Underground, or the many, many crimes she and her cohorts committed. Nor was there any indication that she was ready to repudiate the political ideas and communities that had led to those crimes. In fact, like Boudin and Rosenberg, Clark depended on these same communities to join the *Times* in pressuring authorities to secure her release.

Evans, Rosenberg, Boudin, and Clark all claimed they made their "mistakes" because of their passion for social justice for African-Americans. But if that had been their interest rather than a self-aggrandizing quest for revolutionary authenticity and national notoriety, they would have invested their talents and time in supporting honest, law-abiding, productive African-Americans who by the 1980s were making enormous strides towards equality with others through the democratic process and the economic marketplace. Instead, they declared war on "Amerikkka," planted bombs, rented getaway cars, and served as decoys and lookouts for a gang of criminals who left a path of broken lives in their wake as they robbed banks and armored cars and murdered law enforcement officials, several of whom were African-Americans themselves. What motivated these radicals was not idealism. It was what motivates all violent individuals: a rage welling up from psychic depths, whose causes are not political and which they are the last ones able to identify or understand.

CHAPTER FIVE

Liberated Woman

Man was created a rebel; and how can rebels be happy?
—Ivan Karamazov

When I close my eyes and think of Susan, it is thirty-five years ago and she is coming out of Peter Collier's office at *Ramparts*, the radical magazine whose staff I have only recently joined. The *Ramparts* suite is situated near Fisherman's Wharf in the San Francisco marina, and the room we are standing in is drenched in the salt light reflecting off the Bay. Peter and Susan are engaged in an animated discussion about the article she is writing, which is itself a reflection of the radical adventures in which we are all involved and which engage our innocence and our yet unbroken dreams of finer worlds to come. It is Peter who has come up with the title for the article: "The Politics of The Orgasm." When it appears in the next issue of the magazine, it will provide Susan with her fifteen minutes of fame.

Black-eyed and raven-haired, Susan is handsome enough at twenty-seven to spark a mischievous banter among the office men. This gossip subsides whenever she arrives (as she often does) with her infant daughter Shuna astride her hip, which transforms the mother into a sibling the males suddenly want to protect. As a family man diffident in such matters, I remain an outsider to the sexual chatter. Susan is a married woman, but that does not seem to inhibit her flirtatious energy. Her husband, Michael Lydon, is a writer of some note among us as a former staff reporter for *Newsweek*. Susan has the more artistic temperament, which makes her husband's cachet with the editors a recurring trial when they pass her over to assign him stories about the musical culture, a beat she regards as more properly hers.

These memories of Susan are always a pleasure because her eyes are so full of happiness. Or so it seemed to me at the time. As with many images we encounter, particularly when we are young and inexperienced, there is a lot that remains unseen. In all the pictures of Susan that play in my head from that time, there is no hint of the withering self-doubt buried in the shadows of those vulnerable eyes, or the tsunami of pain that was about to engulf her.

These thoughts were triggered by a phone call I received from a mutual friend with the news that Susan was dead. The cause was cancer of the liver, the third appearance of the disease that had ravaged her in the space of a decade. It had finally vanquished a spirit that seemed invincible, ending her odyssey at the age of sixty-one.

There were obituaries in the *Oakland Tribune* and the *San Francisco Chronicle* and, as I discovered to my mounting amazement, the Associated Press, the *New York Times*, the *Los Angeles Times*, the *Dallas News*, the London *Guardian*, the London *Telegraph*, and even *Die Welt* and *Nouvel Observateur*.

"Susan Lydon 61: Author of Influential Feminist Essay"
(*Los Angeles Times*)

"Susan Lydon: Feminist writer who launched the debate
on the female orgasm" (London *Guardian*)

"Susan Gordon Lydon, a founding editor of *Rolling Stone*
Magazine, who wrote a benchmark feminist essay and
turned her drug addiction into a memoir, has died" (AP)

This was attention suited to a writer of far greater achievement
than Susan, who was hardly a feminist theorist. And it was all due
to the fragment of political correctness she had produced at the
outset of her journey. Every tribute to her without exception
began with the eight-page *Ramparts* article whose subject Peter
had suggested and whose title he had composed. In a further irony
to what was being presented as an epoch-making piece, Susan had
complained at the time that the article had been hidden by the
editors in the back of the book, so little did they think of it. Yet
now, the little piece she had written for *Ramparts* had become her
headstone.

A more reliable truth about the article would have been that it
was an anomaly in Susan's work. Susan was an un-political writer
who would have lived an un-political life but for the environment
around her. Her *Ramparts* piece was no path-breaking work and had
not launched the debate on the female orgasm as the obituary writers
claimed. It was, at best, a modest summary of ideas already current
in the feminist left, and not even a primary interest for Susan, which
is why it originated in a suggestion from Peter. The claim itself—that

the "clitoral orgasm" was equal in importance to the "vaginal orgasm" was not the least bit an idea to which she could lay claim. As she explained in the article itself, the debate about orgasms had been raging for decades. Alfred Kinsey had championed the "progressive" view that Susan merely repeated. Moreover, years before (as she also noted), the sex-researchers Masters and Johnson had established that there was no difference physiologically speaking between the two orgasms, so one could not be superior to the other.

Nonetheless, the eulogist for England's leftwing *Guardian* summarized Susan's life in this portentous sentence: "She raised the issue of the central role of the clitoris in women's sexual fulfillment, and dared to suggest that women do not need men at all to achieve orgasm." In fact, it was a daring achievement only to those who lived in the ideological bubble of the left, and who apparently thought that women were unable to figure such things out for themselves. Obituaries whose intent was to glorify Susan's death as a feminist icon had ended up by trivializing her life.

Reading Susan's article today I am struck by how alien it is to the voice she subsequently developed, which was richly aware of the messy complexities of an actual life. By contrast, the *Ramparts* piece relied on the reality-flattening clichés of the political world we all inhabited: "In retrospect, particularly with the additional perspective of our own time, Freud's theory of feminine sexuality appears an historical rationalization of the Victorian society." She wrote this even though Freud's views on the matter were written well after the Victorian era. Serving the "ethos" of Victorian society, her article went on, Freud developed a "psychology that robbed Victorian women of possible politics." What could this *mean*? Only a political sentimentalist could imagine that the words Freud wrote in "Three Essays on The Theory of Sexuality" had any effect on ordinary women. It was the same delusion that led us at *Ramparts* to think that an article like Susan's could advance women's "liberation."

In the end, the press notices were not really about Susan but about the obituary writers themselves. Through her death, they were paying homage to a political movement whose agendas they shared and which made them feel important. In this attempt to appropriate the meaning of Susan's life, they were abetted by people who had known her, including *Ramparts* editor Robert Scheer. It was Scheer who in making assignments had constantly passed over Susan in favor of her better-known husband, Michael, and it was he who had consigned the famous article to *Ramparts'* back pages. But now Scheer jumped on the death-wagon, boasting to the *Guardian* that Susan's back of the book piece about orgasms was "one of the most important articles ever published in the magazine. It went from being a giggle to a cause."

These reactions brought to mind the memorial service for my father twenty years earlier, where political friends who had known him for half a century could not remember any details of the life he had actually lived but only the political gestures with which they were all associated, and which imparted significance to their existence. Like the obituary writers who could not remember Susan, their purpose was not to honor a person's memory but to serve a cause that made them feel important. This was why Susan's obituaries failed to appreciate her life, preferring to deal with it, *sotto voce*, as something that embarrassed them.

––––

Shortly after her *Ramparts* article was published, Susan began a descent into an underworld of drugs, pursuing a career of self-abasement and abuse that eventually deprived her of everything she had.

It started out as a conventional Sixties adventure when she began an affair with a handsome *Ramparts* mailroom worker named Tuck (as it happened, Scheer's brother-in-law). "Naively, I believed that Michael would tolerate my sexual experimentation," she explained in a memoir she wrote long after, which she called *Take the Long Way Home.*

Susan had belonged to a women's liberation group in Berkeley, which included Scheer's wife and the wives of others in the *Ramparts* circle. The "consciousness-raising" sessions of the group were devoted to flaying the patriarchal oppressions each allegedly suffered at the hands of their romantic partners or spouses. "Some of our friends had open marriages," Susan recalled, "[and] we'd all talked endlessly about smashing monogamy and the nuclear family," which gave an obvious license to her extramarital fling with Tuck. But when Susan confessed her affair to Michael, he failed to be impressed by her liberated behavior and was deeply wounded instead. "As usual," Susan wrote in her memoir, "our misplaced idealism failed miserably when confronted by the explosive feelings of infidelity engendered in our partners; and my marriage, like the relationships of all my sisters in the women's group, fell apart." To avoid confronting her guilt, and instead of attempting to save her young family, Susan picked a fight with Michael and left him for Tuck, confident that she was striking a blow for herself.

In writing about this episode in her memoir, Susan holds herself accountable for what she did, voicing a perspective that could be called her second thoughts: "I could say it was historical pressures of the times, the giddy excitement and revolutionary fervor that accompanied the beginnings of the women's movement, or how casually people fell in and out of relationships in those halcyon days before AIDS. But I have close friends whose marriages survived those times, so I wonder about my own. My behavior was impulsive and self-centered…; like an addict I wanted what I wanted when I wanted it, and damn the consequences." Susan left Michael in January 1969, just shy of her fourth wedding anniversary, and moved in with Tuck, who lived a city away, taking their child Shuna with her. Her lover had no more regard for consequences than Susan did, nor any intention of taking on responsibility for the young family he had broken up. Within six months, Susan was having regrets and seeking reconciliation with her husband, which he rejected. Three months later, while Susan was on a trip to New York, Tuck took the opportunity of her absence to invite another woman into her bed. In retaliation, she had an affair with Tuck's best friend, another roustabout in the *Ramparts* orbit. When the affair became known, which was almost at once, the two men decided to go off on a year-long, round-the-world sailing trip, leaving Susan and little Shuna to fend for themselves.

Susan's next coupling was with the drummer from the rock band "Big Brother and the Holding Company," who introduced her to heroin, the drug that had already killed the band's lead singer, Janis Joplin. By then, Susan had been using drugs of one kind or another for ten years. In her memoir she describes the beginning of her addictions with marijuana at Vassar, which soon ran the gamut of chemical highs, which in the radical ethos of the time were viewed as "mind-expanding" and therefore "liberating." Three years after becoming addicted to heroin, Susan contracted hepatitis, a severely debilitating disease. While ill in bed she received a call from the New York editor of a newsletter published by Arica, a popular school of spiritualism founded by Oscar Ichazo. Susan was a member of Arica, and the editor was calling to say he was leaving his position and wanted Susan to take the editor's job. "I can't come," she told him. "I'm a junkie. I've got hepatitis." "That's okay," he said good-naturedly.

'Just come when you feel better.'" It was as though she had a bad hangover from alcohol. Such was the revolutionary spirit of the times.

The Arica editor became one of Susan's many lovers and gave her a meditation to help heal her liver by "breathing in dark green." Within a month Susan was feeling better, and a blood test confirmed her recovery, although the damage hepatitis does to the liver is never really repaired and the patient never fully recovers. What lesson had she learned? The addict's lesson: "Now that I knew it was safe to get high, I went all-out on a farewell binge with a vengeance."

To outsiders, heroin addiction is a sordid but also boring affair, an orgy of self-absorption and self-destruction. In the natural course of an addicted life, no human bond is left unbroken, no depth of self-degradation unplumbed, and no lesson ever learned. In fifteen years of self-inflicted torment, Susan went through all the stations of its terrible cross: prostitution, battery by lovers, abandonment of family, abortions (five), stealing, stealing from family, drug dealing ("copping" for others), jail terms, rehab sessions, relapses, lies and more lies, and numbing repetitions of the same. "The past few months," she wrote of her failed stay at a rehab facility in Minnesota,

> had been my roughest ever: I'd been raped, robbed, jilted, degraded, demoralized and hit what I thought was really the bottom, turning tricks with freaks.... Sometimes it seemed that the only way I could ever get free was to kill myself. I'd never seriously OD'd, and I doubted that I could come up with enough money or drugs for an overdose even if I wanted one. Of course someone might shoot me or stab me on the street, or some worker with a grudge against me might give me a hot shot, laced with strychnine or battery acid like they did to people who caused them

trouble or ripped them off;... [But] short of dying there was no way out. The way I saw it, I was bound to the dope; we were in this together, till death did us part.... I still did some things I'd always enjoyed—reading, knitting, shopping for clothes. But the me who did them was a shell.... My inner self had been eroded so gradually over the years by the drugs that, without noticing it, I'd ceased to inhabit my own life or even my body. I liked to get so high that I couldn't feel my body; I'd watch my hands moving at the end of my arms but wouldn't be able to feel them. I'd sought oblivion as a relief from pain, but in the process I'd managed to obliterate myself.

Just how complete this obliteration was she was only able to grasp in the final course of therapy that led to her recovery. In one of the sessions, a counselor forced her to confront the wounds she had inflicted on the one person who loved and depended on her more than any other. "I had claimed that I had no guilty feelings about being a dope fiend all those years. 'What about your child?' she asked..." In response Susan dredged up a terrible scene from memory. The day her daughter graduated from junior high school, she made Susan and Paul, her drug addict partner, promise to take her out for a lobster dinner to celebrate. But it was not to be.

Both Paul and I had been late for the actual graduation, then snuck off while it was happening to go down to Executive [the name of a drug drop] and cop. After the graduation, we drove around in the car all day trying to get money to cop [again] and pay for a lobster dinner. Finally Shuna asked me if she could get out of the car and take the subway home alone. In my mind's eye, I could still see her in her little white-and-blue graduation dress walking by herself to the subway. Suddenly the floodgates burst, releasing a torrent of sorrow and guilt from a bottomless well of grief. Sobs tore out of me in spasms that rocked my entire body.

Not long after Shuna's graduation, I visited Susan in New York. It was the first time we had been together since our encounters at *Ramparts* nearly fifteen years before. I knew about her addiction, which was part of the reason I was curious to see her. My own life had been derailed by a collision with the dark side of the political community we had belonged to and had burdened me with a depression from which I feared for a long time I would never be released. Two broken lives made for a kind of kinship. By the time we met, I had begun to turn a corner towards recovery and hoped my experience would be helpful to her. In the time we spent together, we shared our separate miseries, and I did my best to encourage her to look ahead. When we parted, I left with two forebodings. First, I had seen in her eyes a depth of despair that made me wonder whether a recovery for her was really possible. Second, I knew that if she had any chance at health, I could not be part of it, and I would probably never see her again.

The political community in which we had met, with which I had finally collided, was now the only community she had to turn to. There was an irony in this, because Susan's life appeared to me a refutation of everything they believed in. She had been born to all the advantages a society could provide, and natural gifts to go with them. If even individuals with such supports were capable of ruining their lives and wounding others in the process, how did radicals propose to drain the swamp of human misery by redistributing wealth and changing social institutions?

A few years after our meeting, Susan called me. By then she was on the road to health and had completed the memoir of her addiction. She was calling for advice about promoting her memoir, which would soon be off the press. I advised her as best I could, and discussed with her the fact that I would not be able to give her a blurb to help her find an audience. She had returned to Berkeley and a community to whom I was a pariah and my name anathema. I did not want to do anything that would divide her in the slightest from people she needed, and who would be unable to rise above their wars, or separate the personal from the political. I wished her well and said what I knew was my last goodbye.

————

She lived another ten years before the notices of her death brought her back into view and made me want to recover the memories of her that time had obscured. In the intervening years, she had written two more books, which formed an autobiographical trilogy with her memoir. They described the painful journey she had made into the heart of herself and the new life she had created out of the ruins of her past. In *Take the Long Way Home*, she relived the humiliation and guilt of her years of addiction in order to share the secrets of her recovery. The rules were simple: honesty, accountability, and the caring for others that can only begin with the caring for self. The two new books she had written were about the ancient craft that had become her healing art, which was knitting. In these books she entered an uncharted literary terrain, drawing on the threads of continuity in her life: her family, her spiritual training with Arica, and the craft of knitting that had been passed down through the generations of Goldenbergs (her family name), who had been furriers and tailors in the *shtetls* of Europe.

The threads were woven into a narrative whose timeless themes were the same as those of Shakespeare's late romances, which I had studied as a young man in college: reunion, reconciliation, and redemption. "Follow the thread, the circle, the web, the pattern that winds through a life," she wrote in a book she called *The Knitting Sutra*. Follow the thread and integrate your life. Susan had arrived at an integration of the parts of her life whose fragmentation had caused her so much misery before. "*Sutra*, comes from *suture*, which means thread, a connective cord," her text explained. She felt she had followed such a cord "to the center of my being.... When I re-emerged, I was traveling a path of my own making. I had become a person ... who owns myself."

The tone of her writing was also new. No longer driven by the compulsive frenzies of a trapped life, her prose in the *Sutra*, which she subtitled *Craft as a Spiritual Practice*, had a sacramental quality, as a hymn to human possibilities. "I've always liked the saying *Laborare est orare*, work is prayer.... If we are indeed made in the image of our Creator... we are most like that creator when we are creating something ourselves. So the very act is sacred, from the most humble piecing of fabric for a patchwork quilt to the soaring stonework of the great Gothic cathedrals."

Her new vocation had been launched quite unpremeditatedly as the result of an accident. In 1992, while watching a humming bird through binoculars in the Napa Valley, she fell off a friend's deck, fracturing her arm. While the bone was knitting, the doctor recommended that she exercise her hand to prevent the small muscles from atrophying. It was this unforeseeable circumstance that prompted her to revive an old passion and launch her career as a knitter. Citing E. M. Forster's epigraph to *Howards End*—"Only connect"—Susan wrote: "Knitting connects. It connects us to one another. It connects us to our deepest selves, to the vastness of our ancestral knowledge and internal landscape.... Humble though it is, I believe knitting has within it the power to connect heaven with earth. And ... when heaven and earth unite, what happens is a profound and enduring peace." It was the title of her final book, *Knitting Heaven and Earth*.

During her last decade, Susan was in the habit of going to the Russian River every year at the end of July, the month, as it turned out, in which she would die. At the river she would stay in a cabin with a group of her women friends. She would bring her binoculars to watch the ospreys, and her laptop to write her book, and of course her bag of knitting. On one occasion there was a shawl knit from a fiber called *quivit* in her bag. The fiber was "spun from the downy under hair of the musk ox, a shaggy Arctic beast that roams the frozen tundra and puts one in mind of a stubbier, smaller version of the woolly mammoth." The natural color of the fiber is taupe brown, but the skeins in the garment Susan was knitting had come from the fleece of several animals, so that they did not quite match in the color or feel of the thread, creating a variegated fabric.

In her Russian River retreat, Susan used the quivit to knit a lace shawl in a pattern known as "feather and fan," which she had seen wrapped around a baby in a catalogue photograph. "A shawl," she observes "envelops the person in warmth," which has led to the creation of prayer shawl ministries around the country, in which groups knit for members in distress, "stitching their work with prayer" and wrapping the recipients in the shawls "as a blessing." One of her river friends, a woman of Mexican origin named Theresa, fell in love with the finished quivit shawl and purchased it from Susan. "I don't know what I ever did to deserve anything as beautiful as this," she said when she put it on. "This is the sort of thing that I want to be wearing in my open casket."

Later, Theresa told Susan that she had loaned the shawl to her mother who was suffering from lymphoma, because she thought "the shawl might ease the pain of the tumors in her neck." Susan knew that Theresa's mother was accustomed to finery, "nylon hose and immaculate Ferragamos," which made her think: "Now she has a shaggy, imperfect, hand-stitched shawl to warm the achings of her heart and her neck. And since the shawl has a life of its own, like a child you've given birth to, she will probably never know it comes to her courtesy of the great, shambling Arctic beasts whose coats provided the yarn, and of the nimble fingers of the knitter that was me."

In 1994, Susan was diagnosed with renal cancer and had to have her kidney removed. Eight years later, she was diagnosed with breast cancer and had to undergo surgery, radiation, and chemotherapy, which made her sick and caused her to lose her hair. Through her ordeal she held onto the center of gravity she had discovered through her earlier trials, and approached her mortality with dignity and grace. "I don't believe there's a heaven, an afterlife for the good, a paradise of sensual pleasure that the bad are forbidden. I believe in the life that lives in the universe and sky. I believe that we are connected to a larger whole, that we contain within ourselves a spark of divinity. I believe we reincarnate from one body to another, cycling through history and time." Like the musk ox and Theresa's dying mother, connected into one tapestry of life through Susan's quivit shawl.

In April 2004, just when the chemo and radiation treatments had ended and a feeling of normality had begun to return to her, Susan was diagnosed with her third cancer. This time it had invaded her liver and there would be no reprieve. She died in the bosom of her family a month after her last book was published, and having made her final peace. "My life has taken on an exalted quality," she wrote shortly before the end. "Finally I value deeply the time I have. I am grateful for the days out of the hospital... I am thankful to be alive. I have moments of sheer happiness sometimes, when nothing particularly memorable is happening. These moments of joy rise from nowhere and sweep over me like a gentle tide." The cancer had reduced her life to a stark simplicity. "What was left after everything else was swept away was my love for the people with a claim on my heart, my respect for nature, and the healing power of craft: writing, knitting, needlepoint."

Years before she had connected the last remaining thread from the fabric of the life she had so recklessly shredded in the time of her chaos. Like all recovering addicts, part of her discipline was to attend meetings and share with other addicts her story and, with it, the miracle—the practical and obtainable miracle—of her recovery and rebirth. "It was a candlelight meeting, and as soon as they turned out the lights, the energy in the room was transformed.... I shared, as they say, my experience, strength and hope.... Not long ago, I'd been sitting in a program like this one, hoping, but not quite believing that I too could have a better life. Now I was telling others just like me that it was possible. I was living proof. I knew just how they felt; I'd been there too."

When she finished, her daughter Shuna, who was now in her late thirties and had become a pastry chef at Berkeley's famous restaurant, Chez Panisse, came up to her mother and sat in her lap and said: "Every time I hear you speak I'm amazed.... You know, Mom, I feel really honored to be your daughter. When people used to tell me, 'Your mother is a great woman,' I'd think to myself, 'Oh sure, you don't know her like I do.' But now I see why they said it. You are a great woman. And I hope I grow up to be just like you."

This was a woman for each of us to remember. What she achieved in her life was a modest liberation, but an authentic one.

CHAPTER SIX

A Radical Machiavelli

"We are five days away from fundamentally transforming the United States of America."

—Barack Obama

Conservative outlooks spring from observations about the past and as a rule, therefore, are pragmatic. Whatever "first principles" comprise such beliefs, they are (or should be) propositions that encapsulate the lessons of experience. Conservative principles are about limits, and what the respect for limits makes possible. By contrast, progressive views are built on expectations about the future. Progressive principles are based on ideas about a world that does not exist. For progressives, the future is not a maze of human uncertainties and unintended consequences, but a moral choice. To achieve "social justice" requires only that enough people will it.

This ambition leads to several unsavory consequences. First among them is an intolerance for beliefs that question its optimism.

Such beliefs appear as obstacles to the progressive result, and therefore as reactionary and immoral. Second, whereas conservatives defend ideals they believe have led to present good, the ideals progressives defend belong to a future that is only imagined. The significant impact of progressive attitudes lies in the negative stance they take towards the present reality. To annihilate this present is the practical goal of utopian desires. A fundamental aspect of the progressive aspiration is thus the disloyalty it inspires towards the actual communities its adherents inhabit. As the progressive philosopher Richard Rorty observed in a moment of candor: "You have to be loyal to a dream country, rather than one you wake up to every morning."[1]

By calling the progressive future a "dream country," Rorty underscored the dilemma confronting modern radicals who have given up trying to describe the society of the future with which they propose to replace the one they are bent on destroying. Marx scorned nineteenth-century utopians because their ideas were based on wishful thinking. He regarded his version of socialism as "scientific" because its promised future was not a "dream country" but an inevitable outcome of the historical process. By the middle of the twentieth century this Marxist illusion had become increasingly untenable; with the collapse of the Communist system, its "science" became impossible even for progressives to credit. Consequently, they were faced with the dilemma of how to carry on a crusade that had led to such destructive consequences in the absence of a concrete plan to avoid them. The dilemma was resolved by an American radical named Saul Alinsky, whose influence eventually spread to so broad a spectrum of activists that it extended from former Weatherman radical Bill Ayers to his long-time friend and political collaborator Barack Obama, and captured the heart of the Democratic Party itself.

By profession Saul Alinsky was a "community organizer," but like everything else in his political life the term was a calculated camouflage for his real agenda, which was a world-transforming revolution (the original title of his most famous book was *Rules for Revolution*). Alinsky's preferred identification was "rebel," and his entire career was devoted to the destruction of America's social order, which he regarded as oppressive and unjust, and—in his words—worthy of "burning."[2]

Alinsky came of age in the 1930s, where he was drawn to the world of the gangsters he encountered while doing field studies as a graduate student in sociology at the University of Chicago. Alinsky sought out and became a social intimate of the Al Capone mob and its enforcer Frank Nitti, who became the gang's leader when Capone was sent to prison for tax evasion in 1931. Later Alinsky said, "[Nitti] took me under his wing. I called him the Professor and I became his student."[3] While Alinsky was not unmindful of the fact that criminals were dangerous, as a good leftist he held "society"—and in particular, capitalist society—responsible for creating them. In Alinsky's view criminality was not a character problem but a product of the social environment, and in particular the system of private property and individual rights, which radicals like him were determined to abolish.

Alinsky's career as an organizer spanned a period in which the Communist Party loomed as a major force on the American left. Although he never joined the Party, his attitude towards Communists was fraternal, and he regarded them as political allies. In the 1969 "Afterword" to his book *Reveille for Radicals*, he explained his attitude in these words: "Communism itself is irrelevant. The issue is whether they are on our side."[4] Alinsky's failure to oppose communism extended to the Soviet regime. His biographer describes him as an "anti-anti Communist," and his benevolent attitude towards leftwing totalitarians contrasted dramatically with the extreme terms in which he was willing to condemn his own country.

A fraternal approach to the Communists was not universal on the left at the time. In the 1930s, when Alinsky was starting out, Communists played a formative role in creating the CIO, the progressive coalition of industrial unions led by John L. Lewis and then Walter Reuther. But as the Cold War began, and the Red Army started to topple regimes in Eastern Europe, Reuther purged the Communists from the CIO. Reuther was a socialist but—unlike Alinsky—a militant anti-Communist and an American patriot. It is instructive that in *Rules for Radicals*, Alinsky, a deracinated Jew, refers to the exclusion of Communists, who were in practice Soviet agents, as a "Holocaust," a reference offensive to both Jews and to Americans, whose democratic society was under siege. No Communist was sent to a death camp in the McCarthy era, and only a handful of Communist leaders ever spent time in jail for their seditious activities and collaboration with America's enemies.

Like the generation of leftists who came of age after the Soviet collapse, Alinsky understood there were flaws in the Communist outlook. But like those leftists, he never really examined what the flaws might be. He never questioned Marxism's fundamental view of society and human nature, or its goal of a socialist future, and never examined its connection to the epic crimes that Marxists committed. Alinsky never asked himself whether the vision of a society that was socially equal was itself the wellspring of the totalitarian state.

Instead, he identified the problem of communism as one of inflexibility and "dogmatism," proposing as a solution that radicals should be "political relativists" and opportunists, taking a flexible view of the means for achieving their ends. The revolutionary's task, as Alinsky saw it, was first to undermine the existing system and then see what happened (which was exactly Lenin's prescription in Russia). As a consequence, the guidelines Alinsky provided for activists were exclusively devoted to destroying the old order. No thought was given to ensuring that the result did not lead to totalitarian ends or greater oppression. He conceived the radical goal to be singular in purpose: to take power from the "Haves" so that it might be justly redistributed. But he devoted no attention in his work to how a just redistribution might be accomplished without creating a totalitarian state.

Consequently, while his teaching might appear on the surface as "idealism," its prescriptions are deeply problematic. It is a declaration of war on a democracy whose individual freedoms are rooted in the institutions of private property, due process, and limited government, all of which his prescriptions would destroy. Moreover, who are the "people" in whose name his revolution would act—and act without these constraints? History tells us that once the revolution is set in motion, "the people" is whomever the revolutionary elite designates, which is invariably itself.

To advance his political agendas, Alinsky created "community organizations," including a training institute for organizers called the "Industrial Areas Foundation." But his real influence came through his role as the Lenin of the post-Sixties left. Alinsky's work became the practical guide for progressives who had supported Communist causes during the Cold War and were demoralized when the socialist fantasy collapsed, and who needed a theory that would enable them to regroup for a renewed assault on the capitalist foe.

Alinsky wove the inchoate theories of the post-Communist left into a coherent strategy of political organizing. His vision helped to forge the coalition of Communists, anarchists, liberals, Democrats, black racialists, and social justice activists who comprised the post-Cold War left. This left launched the "anti-globalization" movement just before 9/11, and the anti-Iraq War movement just after, and mobilized their forces to help elect one of their own to the White House in 2008—as it happens, a twenty-year Alinsky disciple. As Barack Obama put it at the height of his presidential campaign: "We are the ones we've been waiting for."[5]

Alinsky's political strategy contrasted with that of Sixties radicals who had advanced their revolution "in the streets," and rejected the Democratic Party as a Trojan Horse, which threatened to co-opt their agendas. They did not seek to infiltrate the institutions of American society and government. Tactically, they were confrontationalists. "Up Against the Wall" and "The Sky's the Limit" were their characteristic slogans, and mass protests their preferred form of action. By contrast, Alinsky urged radicals to infiltrate the Democratic Party and traditional institutions with the goal of subverting them. Rhetorical moderation was his stock in trade. While Tom Hayden and Abbie Hoffman were marching on Lyndon Johnson's Pentagon ("Hey, hey, LBJ, how many kids did you kill today?") and fomenting riots at the Democratic convention, Alinsky's organizers were insinuating themselves into Lyndon Johnson's "War on Poverty" program, directing federal funds into their own organizations and causes, and signing up as Democratic Party activists.

The Sixties left had no connection to the labor movement, but Alinsky did. The most important radical labor organizer of the time, United Farmworkers leader Cesar Chavez, was trained by Alinsky and worked for him for ten years. Alinsky's confrontations were not preparations to overthrow the state but were designed as bargaining chips to secure a bigger piece of the pie and gain leverage for the next round. When racial unrest erupted in Rochester, New York, activists called on Alinsky to help them pressure Kodak to hire blacks, a form of racial extortion that foreshadowed the direction of civil rights activism in the era of Jesse Jackson and Al Sharpton.

Alinsky also pioneered the alliance of radicals with the Democratic Party, which ended two decades of hostile conflict that climaxed in the convention riot of 1968. Alinsky was appalled by the riot. Radicals should not be warring against Democrats in the streets, he wrote, but organizing to become the delegates inside the convention hall.[6] Through Chavez, Alinsky had met Robert Kennedy (who supported his muscling of Kodak executives), who was one of the avenues through which Alinsky organizers made their way into the inner circles of the Democratic Party.

In 1969, the year that publishers reissued Alinsky's first book, *Reveille for Radicals*, a Wellesley undergraduate named Hillary Rodham submitted a 92-page research project on Alinsky for her senior thesis.[7] In her conclusion Clinton compared Alinsky to Eugene Debs, Walt Whitman, and Martin Luther King, as someone who was considered dangerous not because he was a self-declared enemy of the American system, but because he "embraced the most radical of political faiths—democracy."

The title of Clinton's thesis was "There Is Only the Fight: An Analysis of the Alinsky Model." In this title she had identified the single most important Alinsky contribution to the radical cause: his embrace of political nihilism. An SDS radical once wrote, "The issue is never the issue. The issue is always the revolution."[8] In other words, the cause of a political action—whether civil rights or women's rights—is never the real cause; women, blacks, and other "victims" are only instruments in the larger cause, which is power. Battles over rights and other issues, according to Alinsky, should never be seen as more than occasions to advance the real agenda, which is the accumulation of power and resources in radical hands. *Power* is the all-consuming goal of Alinsky's politics.

This focus on power was illustrated by an anecdote recounted in a *New Republic* article that appeared during Obama's presidential campaign: "When Alinsky would ask new students why they wanted to organize, they would invariably respond with selfless bromides about wanting to help others. Alinsky would then scream back at them that there was a one-word answer: 'You want to organize for *power!*'"[9] In *Rules for Radicals*, Alinsky wrote: "From the moment an organizer enters a community, he lives, dreams, eats, breathes, sleeps only one thing, and that is to build the mass power base of what he calls the army."[10] The issue is never the issue. The issue is always building the army. The issue is always the revolution.

Guided by these principles, Alinsky's disciples are misperceived as idealists; in fact, they are practiced Machiavellians. Their focus is invariably on means rather than ends. As a result they are not bound by organizational orthodoxies or theoretical dogmatisms in the way their still admired Marxist forebears were. Within the framework of their revolutionary agendas, they are flexible and opportunistic and will say anything (and pretend to be anything) to get what they want, which is power.

Communists identified their goal as a "dictatorship of the proletariat," which generated opposition to their plans. Alinsky and his followers organize their power bases without naming their goal, except to describe it in abstract terms like "social justice" and an "open society." They do not commit themselves to specific institutional aims, whether it is the dictatorship of the proletariat or government ownership of the means of production. Instead, they focus on identifying their opponents as "Haves" and the "privileged," and work to build a power base to undermine the existing arrangements based on private property and individual liberty, which lead to social inequalities. By refusing to commit to principles or to identify goals, they are better able to organize coalitions of the disaffected, which otherwise would be divided over the proper means to achieve their ends, and thus accumulate power.

The demagogic banner of Alinsky's revolution is "democracy," as Hillary Rodham observed. But it is not democracy as Americans understand it. Instead it is a radical democracy in which earned hierarchies based on achievement and merit are targeted for destruction. To Alinsky radicals, "democracy" means replacing all those who are in power with representatives of "the people." It is an old, discredited idea recast. Revolutionary elites mobilize the "oppressed" as a battering ram to bring down the system and make their own way to power. The democracy that Alinsky radicals intend is Leninist not Madisonian, a radical leveling of everyone but the revolutionary elite.

When Hillary Clinton graduated from Wellesley in 1969, she was offered a job at Alinsky's training institute in Chicago. She opted instead to enroll at Yale Law School, where she met her husband and future president, William Jefferson Clinton. In March 2007, the *Washington Post* reported that she had kept her connections to the Alinsky network even in the White House: "As first lady," the paper noted, "Clinton occasionally lent her name to projects endorsed by the Industrial Areas Foundation (IAF), the Alinsky group that had offered her a job in 1968."[11]

Unlike Hillary Clinton, Barack Obama never personally met Alinsky, but as a young man became an adept practitioner of his political methods. In 1985 a group of twenty churches in Chicago offered Obama a job helping residents of poor, predominantly black, South Side neighborhoods. The group was part of a network that included the Gamaliel Foundation, which operated on Alinsky principles. Obama became director of the Developing Communities Project, an affiliate of Gamaliel where he worked for the next three years on initiatives that ranged from job training to school reform to hazardous waste cleanup. A reporter who researched the projects sums them up in these words: "The proposed solution to every problem on the South Side was a distribution of government funds…"[12]

Three of Obama's Chicago mentors were trained at the Alinsky Industrial Areas Foundation, and for several years Obama himself taught workshops on the Alinsky methods.[13] Beginning in the mid-1980s, Obama began work as legal counsel for the Alinsky organization, ACORN, soon to become the largest radical organization in the United States.[14] Gregory Galluzzo, one of Obama's three Alinsky mentors, shared his training manual for new organizers with the *New Republic*'s Ryan Lizza, which he said was little different from the version he used to train Obama in the 1980s. According to Lizza, "It is filled with workshops and chapter headings on understanding power: 'power analysis,' 'elements of a power organization,' 'the path to power.' Galluzzo told me that many new trainees have an aversion to Alinsky's gritty approach because they come to organizing as idealists rather than realists. The Alinsky manual instructs them to get over these hang-ups. 'We are not virtuous by not wanting power,' it says. 'We are really cowards for not wanting power,' because 'power is good' and 'powerlessness is evil.'"[15] For Alinsky and his followers, power—a means—is in fact the end.

According to Lizza, who interviewed Obama as well as Galluzzo, "the other fundamental lesson Obama was taught was Alinsky's maxim that self-interest is the only principle around which to organize people. (Galluzzo's manual goes so far as to advise trainees in block letters: 'get rid of do-gooders in your church and your organization.')

Obama was a fan of Alinsky's realistic streak. 'The key to creating successful organizations was making sure people's self-interest was met,' he told me, 'and not just basing it on pie-in-the-sky idealism. So there were some basic principles that remained powerful then, and in fact I still believe in.'" On Barack Obama's presidential campaign website, one could see a photo of Obama in a classroom "teaching students Alinskyan methods. He stands in front of a blackboard on which he has written, 'Power Analysis' and 'Relationships Built on Self-Interest.'"[16]

In 1986, at the age of twenty-three and fresh out of Columbia University, Obama was hired by the Alinsky team "to organize residents on the South Side [of Chicago] while learning and applying Alinsky's philosophy of street-level democracy."[17] From that time until he became an elected legislator in 1996, the focus of his political activities was ACORN. A summary of his ACORN activities was compiled by the *Wall Street Journal*:

> In 1991, he took time off from his law firm to run a voter-registration drive for Project Vote, an Acorn partner that was soon fully absorbed under the Acorn umbrella. The drive registered 135,000 voters and was considered a major factor in the upset victory of Democrat Carol Moseley Braun over incumbent Democratic Senator Alan Dixon in the 1992 Democratic Senate primary.
>
> Mr. Obama's success made him a hot commodity on the community organizing circuit. He became a top trainer at Acorn's Chicago conferences. In 1995, he became Acorn's attorney, participating in a landmark case to force the state of Illinois to implement the federal Motor Voter Law. That law's loose voter registration requirements would later be

exploited by Acorn employees in an effort to flood voter rolls with fake names.

In 1996, Mr. Obama filled out a questionnaire listing key supporters for his campaign for the Illinois Senate. He put Acorn first (it was not an alphabetical list).[18]

After Obama became a U.S. senator, his wife, Michelle, told a reporter, "Barack is not a politician first and foremost. He's a community activist exploring the viability of politics to make change." Her husband commented: "I take that observation as a compliment."[19]

Alinksy dedicates his signature work, *Rules for Radicals*, to the devil, the first rebel: "Lest we forget, an over-the-shoulder acknowledgment to the very first radical: from all our legends, mythology, and history (and who is to know where mythology leaves off and history begins—or which is which), the first radical known to man who rebelled against the establishment and did it so effectively that he at least won his own kingdom—Lucifer."

Thus, at the very outset, Alinsky tells us what a radical is. He is not a reformer of the system, even God's system, but its would-be destroyer. In his own mind the radical is building his own kingdom of heaven on earth. But since a kingdom of heaven built by human beings is an impossible dream, the radical's real world efforts are directed to subverting and destroying the society he lives in. He is a nihilist. In *The 18th Brumaire* Marx summed up the radical passion by appropriating a comment made by Goethe's Mephistopheles: "Everything that exists deserves to perish."

Alinsky's tribute to Satan reminds us that the radical illusion is an ancient one and has not changed though the millennia. Recall how Satan tempted Adam and Eve to destroy their paradise by telling them that if they ate from the Tree of Knowledge they would be "as God."

This is the radical *hubris*: to create a new race of men and women who are able to live in harmony and according to the principles of social justice. To be as God. Creating such a race requires the total control—the totalitarian control—of individual behavior. Not incidentally, the kingdom the first radical "won," as Alinsky so thoughtlessly puts it, was *hell*. Typical of radicals not to notice the ruin they leave behind.

The book that follows the dedication to Lucifer begins with a friendly critique of the Sixties' New Left. What bothers Alinsky about Sixties radicals is their honesty. While the Old Left—American Communists—pretended to be Jeffersonian Democrats and "progressives," forming "popular fronts" with liberals and infiltrating the Democratic Party, New Left radicals disdained these deceptions, regarding them as a display of inauthenticity and weakness. To distinguish themselves from such popular front politics, Sixties radicals said to anyone who was listening that they were *revolutionaries* and proud of it.

New Left radicals despised liberals, staging riots at Democratic Party conventions. Slogans like "Up against the wall motherf---er" and "Off the Pig" telegraphed exactly how they felt about those who opposed them. Alinsky's chief advice to practitioners of what he regarded as infantile tactics is to *lie* to their opponents, instead—to disarm them by pretending to be moderates and liberals and willing to work with them. He complained about Sixties activists that they were "one moment reminiscent of the idealistic early Christians yet they also urge violence and cry, 'Burn the system down!' They have no illusions about the system, but plenty of illusions about the way to change our world. It is to this point that I have written this book."[20] In other words, the system—the American system—should be burned to the ground, but to achieve this goal you must conceal your intentions. Conceal the goal and you can accomplish anything.

According to Alinsky, it is important for radicals to deal with the world as it is: "As an organizer I start where the world is, as it is, not as I would like it to be. That we accept the world as it is does not in any sense weaken our desire to change it into what we believe it should be—it is necessary to begin where the world is if we are going to change it to what we think it should be. That means working in the system."[21] It was with these Alinsky lines that Michelle Obama chose to sum up her husband's vision at the Democratic convention that nominated him for president. Referring to a visit he had made to Chicago neighborhoods, she said, "And Barack stood up that day, and he spoke words that have stayed with me ever since. He talked about 'the world as it is' and 'the world as it should be.' And he said that, all too often, we accept the distance between the two and we settle for the world as it is, even when it doesn't reflect our values and aspirations. But he reminded us that we also know what our world should look like. He said we know what fairness and justice and opportunity look like. And he urged us to believe in ourselves, to find the strength within ourselves to strive for the world as it should be. And isn't that the great American story?"[22] It was pitch-perfect Alinskyism.

As president, Barack Obama appointed Van Jones to be his "special assistant" for "green jobs," a key position in his plans for America's future. According to his account, Van Jones became a Communist during a prison term he served after being arrested during the 1992 Los Angeles race riots. For the next ten years, he was an activist in the Maoist organization STORM, whose acronym means "Stand Together to Organize a Revolutionary Movement." When STORM disintegrated, Jones joined the Apollo Alliance, an environmental coalition organized by Alinsky radicals, which subsequently played a major role in designing Obama's green programs. He also joined the Center for American Progress, a brain trust for the Democratic Party headed by John Podesta, former White House chief of staff in the Clinton administration and co-chair of Obama's transition team.

In a 2005 interview, Van Jones explained to a reporter that he still considered himself a "revolutionary, but just a more effective one." "Before," he said, "we would fight anybody, any time. No concession was good enough.... Now, I put the issues and constituencies first. I'll work with anybody, I'll fight anybody if it will push our issues forward.... *I'm willing to forgo the cheap satisfaction of the radical pose for the deep satisfaction of radical ends*"(emphasis added).[23] It was an embodiment of the Alinsky doctrine.

"These rules," wrote Alinsky, "make the difference between being a realistic radical and being a rhetorical one who uses the tired old words and slogans, calls the police 'pig' or 'white fascist racist' or 'motherf---er and has so stereotyped himself that others react by saying, 'Oh, he's one of those,' and then promptly turn off."[24] Instead, advance your radical goals by camouflaging them.

There is nothing new in the strategy of appearing moderate in order to disarm your opposition. It was Lenin's idea, too, which is where Alinsky found it. Thus Alinsky turns to Lenin in the course of chiding rhetorical radicals of the Sixties over one of their favorite slogans (appropriated from the Chinese Communist dictator Mao Zedong). Comments Alinsky: "'Power comes out of the barrel of a gun' is an absurd rallying cry when the other side has all the guns. Lenin was a pragmatist; when he returned to what was then Petrograd from exile, he said that the Bolsheviks stood for getting power through the ballot but would reconsider after they got the guns."[25]

Lenin may have been a pragmatist, but only within the parameters of the revolution. He was a dogmatist in theory and a Machiavellian in practice. He was always engaged in a total war, which he used to justify every means he thought might advance his goals. These included summary executions, concentration camps that provided a model for Hitler, and the physical "liquidation" of entire social classes. Lenin was the most dangerous kind of political fanatic—ready to resort to any means to get what he wanted, even if it meant pretending to be a democrat.

"[The] failure of many of our younger activists to understand the art of communication has been disastrous," Alinsky wrote. What he really meant was their *honesty* was disastrous—their failure to understand the art of *mis*-communication. This is the art he taught to radicals trying impose socialism on a country whose people understand that socialism destroys freedom: Don't sell it as socialism. Sell it as "progressivism," "economic democracy," "fairness," and "social justice."

The very first chapter of Alinsky's manual for radicals, in which he proposes to set the framework for what follows, is called "The Purpose." Its epigraph is taken from the Book of Job: "The life of man upon earth is a warfare…" This is hardly an invitation to democratic politics, as understood by the American Founders. The American system was created to achieve compromise and to bring warring factions into a working partnership. The Founders devised a system of checks and balances to temper popular passions and prevent them from cutting each other's throats.

In Alinsky's view the difference between the unethical behavior counseled by Machiavelli and the unethical behavior he would like to see practiced by radicals is merely that their political enemies are different. "*The Prince* was written by Machiavelli for the Haves on how to hold power. *Rules for Radicals* is written for the Have-Nots on how to take it away."[26]

Alinsky and his disciples view America's democracy as a hierarchical society similar to all those that went before it: "The setting for the drama of change has never varied. Mankind has been and is divided into the Haves, the Have-Nots, and Have-a-Little, Want Mores."[27] The claim is another Alinsky theft, in this case from the *Communist Manifesto*, which famously begins, "The history of all hitherto existing society is the history of class struggles" and then describes those struggles: "Freeman and slave, patrician and plebian, lord and serf, guild-master and journeyman, in a word, oppressor and oppressed, stood in constant opposition to one another, carried on an uninterrupted, now hidden, now open fight, a fight that each time ended, either in a revolutionary reconstitution of society at large, or in the common ruin of the contending classes."

This was nonsense when Marx wrote it—and worse, when one considers the tens of millions of individuals slaughtered by those who believed it. But it is the bedrock of radical belief, and the foundation of the left's destructive agendas. The idea that the world is divided into Haves and Have-Nots, exploiters and exploited, oppressors and oppressed, leads directly to the conclusion that liberation lies in the elimination of the former, which is the only way to end such a conflict. According to radicals, this will lead to the liberation of mankind. In fact, it led to the murders of 100 million people in the last century, and state-induced economic deprivation on a scale never witnessed before.

In the myth created by Marx, which all radicals to one degree or another believe, the market system is a zero sum game where one man's gain is another's loss. Because the Haves will defend what is theirs, to achieve justice it is necessary to strip them of privilege and power. That is why radicals are organized for war—a stealth guerilla campaign at the outset, and a total war at the end. The myth of the Haves and the Have-Nots is a secular version of the religious vision of a world divided into Good and Evil. In addition to being followers of Machiavelli, Alinsky radicals are secular Manicheans. If it were true that all the social misery in the world were attributable to the greed and selfishness of one group, radicals would have a righteous case. But the claim is a fiction. Moreover, radicals acting on this claim have themselves been the cause of the greatest human suffering on record.

Consider again the opening lines of the *Communist Manifesto*. The history of all previous societies is the history of "class struggle," of a war between the Haves and the Have-Nots. Marx then names them through time. In Marx's schema, capitalists and business people are in our era the new oppressors, while proletarians—workers—are the new oppressed. Post-Communist radicals have added women, racial minorities, and even sexual minorities to the list of those oppressed, although to compare women and minorities in a democracy to slaves and serfs, and businessmen to slave-owners and feudal lords, is delusional and offensive.

But so are the categories "Haves" and "Have-Nots." There are tens of millions of capitalists in America, and they rise and fall with every economic wave. Where are the Enrons and Lehmans of yesteryear and where are their bosses? If proletarians can become capitalists and capitalists can become paupers, there is no class struggle in the sense that Marx and his acolytes claim, no system of oppression, no Haves and Have-Nots, and no need for revolution. The same is even more obviously the case where racial minorities and women are concerned. In the last decade America has had a black president, two black secretaries of state, three women secretaries of state, a chief law enforcement officer who is black, and so forth and so on. Many of the Fortune 500 companies are headed by women, some of them racial minorities. No slave or serf ever held such positions, or could. The radical creed is a religious myth. And a myth designed to provoke civil war.

In a democracy like America, the notion that there are Haves and Have-Nots is akin to the Manichean view that the world is ruled by Satan and history is a struggle between the ruling forces of darkness and the liberating forces of light. In this radical vision, the "Haves" are a category identical to "witches" in the Puritan faith—agents of the devil—and serve the same purpose for the preachers of this doctrine. The purpose is to identify one's political enemies as instruments of evil and thus to justify the total war against them.

Of course there is a partial truth in this malignant vision, which is the only reason it is possible to sustain it. There are *some* Haves, namely individuals who have inherited wealth and merely have it, as opposed to those who are active investors creating more wealth for themselves and others. There are also *some* Have-Nots, people who were born to nothing and because of character flaws or disabilities or other social dysfunctions have no way of changing their circumstances. But it is false to describe the economic divisions in American society in these terms, or to imply that there are immovable social barriers to individuals seeking to better themselves and increase their wealth. If a person can move from one rung of the ladder to the next, there is no hierarchy in Marx's sense and no premise for revolutionary change.

In the real world of American democracy, social and economic divisions are between the Cans and the Can-Nots, the Dos and the Do-Nots, the Wills and the Will-Nots. The vast majority of wealthy Americans, as a matter of empirical fact, are first generation and have created and earned what they possess. In the process of creating wealth for themselves, they have created wealth for hundreds and sometimes hundreds of thousands of others. But to describe the wealthy as wealth *earners* and wealth *creators*, that is, to describe them accurately, would explode the whole religious fantasy that gives meaning to radical lives.

Because the radical agenda is based on a religious myth, a reader of any radical text, including Alinsky's, will constantly come across statements that are patently absurd. According to Alinsky, "All societies discourage and penalize ideas and writings that threaten the status quo." The statement is again lifted directly from Marx, this time from his *German Ideology*, which claims that "the ruling ideas are the ideas of the ruling class." From this false claim, Alinsky proceeds to the following preposterous conclusion: "It is understandable therefore, that the literature of a Have society is a veritable desert whenever we look for writings on social change." According to Alinsky this is particularly true of American society, which "has given us few words of advice, few suggestions on how to fertilize social change."[28]

On what planet did this man live and do his disciples now agitate to believe such stuff? How could they miss the narratives of "resistance" and "change" which have been familiar themes of our culture and dominant themes of our school curriculums, our presidency, and our political discourse? Alinsky's own book of advice on how to burn the system down is one of the most famous books of the time— recommended reading, in fact, on the official website of the National Education Association. But Alinsky presses on: "From the Haves, on the other hand, there has come an unceasing flood of literature justifying the status quo."

The reality is exactly the reverse. The curriculum of virtually every university department of Women's Studies, Black Studies, Peace Studies, Gay and Lesbian Studies, Asian, Chicano, and Native American Studies, Cultural Studies, American Studies, and also anthropology, sociology, English and Comparative Literature are openly dedicated to social change.[29] The goal of the most prestigious schools of

Education, often incorporated into their formal mission statements, is "social change," and more specifically "social justice." (Bill Ayers has edited a series of instructional guides published by Columbia University on teaching social justice in the classroom.) Promoting social change and social justice have become routine subjects of commencement addresses, which are often given by anti-capitalist radicals such as Angela Davis, Michael Moore, and Bernardine Dohrn. The newest mass medium, the Internet, features popular websites such as Daily Kos, MoveOn.org, and others too numerous to mention, which are dedicated to promoting the Alinsky program of taking wealth and power from the so-called "Haves" in the name of the so-called "Have-Nots." Finally, there is the inconvenient fact that America's first black president, a radical organizer and leader of an Alinsky organization himself, and a lifelong member of the political left, announced on the eve of his election that "we are five days away from fundamentally transforming the United States of America."[30]

Alinsky's approach to political combat is captured in an anecdote provided by Alinsky's sympathetic biographer, Sanford Horwitt, in his book, *Let Them Call Me Rebel*. In this anecdote, Alinsky shared his wisdom with students wishing to protest the appearance on their campus of the first president George Bush, at the time America's representative to the UN during the Vietnam War:

> College student activists in the 1960s and 1970s sought out
> Alinsky for advice about tactics and strategy. On one such
> occasion in the spring of 1972 at Tulane University's
> annual week-long series of events featuring leading public
> figures, students asked Alinsky to help plan a protest of a
> scheduled speech by George Bush, then U.S. representative
> to the United Nations, a speech likely to be a defense of the

Nixon Administration's Vietnam War policies.[31] The students told Alinsky that they were thinking about picketing or disrupting Bush's address. That's the wrong approach, he rejoined—not very creative and besides, causing a disruption might get them thrown out of school.[32] He told them, instead, to go hear the speech dressed up as members of the Ku Klux Klan, and whenever Bush said something in defense of the Vietnam War, they should cheer and wave placards, reading "The K.K.K. supports Bush." And that is what the students did with very successful, attention-getting results.[33]

This vignette illuminates Alinsky's ethics, and in particular his attitude towards means and ends. His model, Lenin, declared that the purpose of a political argument was not to refute one's opponent "but to wipe him from the face of the earth." In Lenin's mind his opponents were agents of evil and had to be destroyed. Alinsky's *modus operandi* is identical. It didn't matter to Alinsky that the Vietnam War was not a race war, or that millions of South Vietnamese opposed the Communists and welcomed the United States, or that the South was eventually conquered and occupied by North Vietnamese armies who turned the country into a prison. It didn't matter to Alinsky who George Bush actually was or what he believed. In a war, the objective is to destroy the enemy—by any means necessary.

Alinsky's recommendation to the student protesters was to take a symbol of one of the greater evils Americans had been associated with, and employ it with the intention of obliterating the memory of everything good America ever did. If America's cause in Vietnam was the Ku Klux Klan, then its cause was evil and America was evil. If George Bush was a spokesman for the Ku Klux Klan, no more need

be said. His destruction was not only justified, it was morally obliga-
tory. In Alinsky's war, the real individual, George Bush, is made to
disappear so that the enemy George Bush can be defeated. These are
the methods of political argument that Lenin perfected and that
radicals have employed ever since.

Consequently, the most important chapter of Alinsky's manual
is titled "Means and Ends." It is designed to address his biggest problem, which is how to explain to idealistic radicals who think of themselves as creating a world of perfect justice and harmony that the
means they must use to achieve that world are dishonest, deceitful,
and ruthless—and therefore indefensible by the moral standards they
claim to be upholding. The radical organizer has no such standards,
Alinsky explains; he "does not have a fixed truth—truth to him is
relative and changing; *everything* to him is relative and changing. He
is a political relativist."[34]

True liberals are not relativists. They may share the radical's utopian agenda of a just and peaceful world, but they also have scruples.
While they support radical ends, their principles cause them to withhold their support when radicals use means that may defeat the ends.
It is because they have scruples that Alinsky's contempt for liberals is
boundless. In his first book, *Reveille for Radicals*, he wrote: "While
liberals are most adept at breaking their own necks with their tongues,
radicals are most adept at breaking the necks of conservatives."[35] In
contrast to liberals, who in Alinsky's eyes are constantly tripping over
their principles, the rule for radicals is straightforward: the ends
justify the means.

It is not because radicals begin by being unethical people that they
approach politics this way. On the contrary, their passion for a future
that is ethically perfect is what drives their political agendas and
causes others to mistake them for idealists. But the very nature of this

future—a world without poverty, without war, without racism, and without "sexism"—is so desirable, so noble, so perfect in contrast to everything that has preceded it as to justify any and every means to make it a reality.

If the radicals' utopia were actually possible, it would be criminal *not* to deceive, to lie, and to murder in order to advance the radical cause. If it were possible to provide every man, woman, and child in the world with food, shelter, and clothing as a right, if it were possible to end bigotry and human conflict, what sacrifice would not be worth it, what crime not justified? The German philosopher Nietzsche had an epigram for this: "Idealism kills." The nobler the cause, the greater the crime it will justify. The great atrocities of the modern era, whether Nazi or Communist, were committed by idealists—people who believed they were saving mankind.

If the goal is to overthrow an existing social order, it is necessary to break its rules. Consequently, to be radical is to be a willing outlaw. During the Sixties, SDS leader Tom Hayden once described the utility of the drug culture, while claiming he was not part of it. Once you get a middle class person to break the law, he said, they are on their way to becoming revolutionaries.[36] In the Sixties, radicals were generally proud of the idea that they were linked to criminals. Gangsters such as John Dillinger and films such as *The Wild Bunch* and *Bonnie and Clyde*, which celebrated American outlaws, were popular among them. Abbie Hoffman's *Steal This Book* was a manifesto of the creed. Obama friend and Weatherman leader Bernardine Dohrn's tribute to the murderer Charles Manson was its extreme expression. This romance with evil continues to be expressed in radicals' affinity for criminals and their causes at home and abroad, as it was in Alinsky's early attraction to Capone's enforcer Frank Nitti, not to mention his dedication to Lucifer.

The Stalinist historian Eric Hobsbawm gave this romance an academic veneer in a book he wrote about Sicilian criminals whom he described as "primitive rebels"—in short, revolutionaries *avant la lettre*. One of the chapters of *Primitive Rebels* is titled "Social Bandits," criminals whom Hobsbawm regarded as avatars of "social justice," their activity "little more than endemic peasant protest against oppression and poverty."[37] In this Hobsbawm showed his contempt for poor people who are law abiding. According to Hobsbawm the activity of the "mob" is "always directed against the rich," and therefore acceptable.[38] The French radical Pierre-Joseph Proudhon also gave license to radicals to steal and destroy by coining socialism's most famous epigraph: "Property is Theft." In reality, of course, it is socialism that is theft.

Alinsky's entire argument is framed as an effort to answer liberals who refuse to join the radical cause, saying, "I agree with your ends but not your means." To this Alinsky replies that the very question, "Does the end justify the means?" is "meaningless." The real question, according to Alinsky, is "Does this particular end justify this particular means?"[39] But even this formulation is at bottom evasive, since radicals are in a permanent war and "the third rule of the ethics of means and ends is that in war the end justifies almost any means."[40]

The sum and substance of Alinsky's lecture about means and ends was originally published forty years earlier in a famous pamphlet by the Bolshevik leader Leon Trotsky. In a pamphlet he called *Their Morals and Ours*, Trotsky explained the revolutionary creed in the course of justifying the bloody crimes that Russia's Communists had already committed.[41] "Whoever does not care to return to Moses, Christ or Mohammed; whoever is not satisfied with eclectic hodge-podges must acknowledge that morality is a product of social development; that there is nothing invariable about it; that it serves social interests; that these interests are contradictory; that morality more than any other form of ideology has a class character." In other words, there is no such thing as morality; there are only class interests—the interests of the Haves versus the Have-Nots. Right for a revolutionary is that which serves the Have-Nots and their cause, however immoral it may seem by commonly accepted standards of right and wrong.

"Whenever we think about social change," Alinsky writes, "the question of means and ends arises. The man of action views the issue of means and ends in pragmatic and strategic terms. He has no other problem." In other words, like Trotsky, Alinsky's radical is not going to worry about the legality or morality of his actions, only their practical effects. If they are seen to advance the cause, they are justified. "[The radical] asks of ends only whether they are achievable and worth the cost; of means, only whether they will work." But how is one to judge whether they work except by the final result—the creation of a perfect future? Doesn't such a course corrupt the cause and shape its outcome? In practice, Marxists killed 100 million people—in peacetime—justifying every step of their way by the nobility of the mission. Their victims were "enemies of the people" and therefore disposable. How to prevent such terrible outcomes except by observing a moral standard?

Alinsky answers the question about corrupt means this way: *everybody does it.* "To say that corrupt means corrupt the ends is to believe in the immaculate conception of ends and principles. The real arena is corrupt and bloody. Life is a corrupting process ... he who fears corruption fears life." In this jaundiced view, there is no one who is not corrupt, who does not lie, cheat, steal, murder; it is all just business as usual. In which case there is no distinction to be made between tolerant democracies and totalitarian dictatorships. In pursuing a radical politics, Alinsky advises, "One does not always enjoy the luxury of a decision that is consistent both with one's individual conscience and the good of mankind. The choice must always be for the latter."[42] But who determines what is good for mankind? In Alinsky's universe there is only the revolutionary elite, and there is no higher court of appeal.

The Russian novelist Dostoevsky famously wrote, "If God does not exist then everything is permitted." What he meant was that if human beings do not believe in a good that is outside themselves, they will act as gods and there will be nothing to restrain them. Alinsky is already there: "Action is for mass salvation and not for the individual's personal salvation. He who sacrifices the mass good for his personal salvation has a peculiar conception of 'personal salvation;' he doesn't care enough for people to be 'corrupted' for them."[43] In other words, the evil that radicals may do is already justified by the fact that they do it for the salvation of mankind—as defined by them.

Notice the scare quotes Alinsky puts around the verb "corrupted," a sign that he does not actually believe in moral corruption, because he does not believe in morality itself. His morality begins and ends with the radical cause. The sadistic dictator Fidel Castro, one of Alinsky's radical heroes, summarized this principle in a famous formulation: "Within the revolution everything is possible; outside the revolution nothing is possible." The revolution—the radical cause— is the way, the truth, and the life.

Beginning with Rousseau and Marx and extending to our own day, revolutionaries have never articulated an actual plan of the future they promise. The utopians who tried to build communities that would institute "social justice" failed. They failed to build just communities, and even failed to build communities that were viable. Revolutionaries like Lenin and Alinsky, who are prepared to burn down existing civilizations and put their opponents to the wall, never have a plan. What they offer is a destructive rage against the worlds they inhabit, and what they provide is an emotional symbol of the future they propose—in Marx's case "the kingdom of freedom," in Alinsky's "the open society." These seductive images are designed to sanction fraud, mayhem, and murder, all justified as necessary to gain passage to the promised land. But revolutionaries never spend a moment thinking about how to make an actual society function: how to keep people from injuring each other; how to motivate them to work; how to provide incentives to those who will actually create wealth.

What if there is no future that can actually fulfill the revolutionary aspiration? Then the means employed to get there are what *make* the revolutionary future. Each step of the way creates a new world—the only new world that human beings can create. What revolutionaries like Lenin and Alinsky offer is not salvation but chaos—a chaos designed to produce a totalitarian state.

The Roman general Scipio Africanus wept when his legions burned Carthage because in its flames he saw the future of his beloved Rome. The ancients did not view history as a progress, but as a series of cycles in which civilizations come into being, rise, and fall. In the biblical story, an angel with a flaming sword stands at the Gates of Eden, preventing God's wayward children from returning to the paradise they abandoned. The fall of Adam and Eve is a parable of the impossibility of an earthly bliss. And could it be otherwise if the world that so obviously needs repair is a world that we ourselves have made? This is the religious view of the circumstances in which we find ourselves; and it is also the conservative view; and it is also mine.

Notes

Introduction

1. As Peter Collier and I noted in our 1989 book about leaving the left, *Destructive Generation*. Lionel Trilling, *The Middle of the Journey*, 1947.

2. Cited in Peter Collier and David Horowitz, *Destructive Generation* (Encounter Books edition, 2005), pp. 375–76.

3. Cf., David Horowitz and Jacob Laksin, *One-Party Classroom: How Radical Professors at America's Top Colleges Indoctrinate Students and Undermine Our Democracy* (Crown, 2009); Robert Bork, *Slouching Towards Gomorrah: Modern Liberalism and American Decline*, 2003.

Chapter One

1. Doug Henwood, "Re: [PEN-L] David Horowitz & Peter Collier host Christopher Hitchens at the Freedom Center," pen-l, June 6, 2007, http://www.mail-archive.com/pen-l@sus.csuchico.edu/msg26336.html.

2. Christopher Hitchens, "The Life of Johnson," *Critical Quarterly*, 1989, FSA, p. 260.

3. Christopher Hitchens, *Hitch-22: A Memoir* (Hachette Book Group, 2010), p. 46 (hereafter *Hitch-22*).

4. Ibid., p. 36.

5. Ibid., p. 7.

6. Ibid.

7. Terry Eagleton, "Hitch-22: A Memoir, by Christopher Hitchens," *New Statesman*, May 31, 2010, http://www.newstatesman.com/books/2010/05/christopher-hitchens-iraq-self.

8. *Hitch-22*, p. 105.

9. David Horowitz, *Radical Son* (Simon & Schuster, 1997), p. 280.

10. *Hitch-22*, p. 22.

11. Ibid., pp. 25–26.

12. I owe these perceptions to my friend Peter Collier.

13. *Hitch-22*, p. 13.

14. Ibid., p. 98.

15. Ibid., p. 87.

16. Peter Hitchens, *The Broken Compass* (Continuum, 2009), p. 75.

17. Ibid.

18. *Hitch-22*, p. 106.

19. Ibid., p. 108.

20. Ibid., p. 181.

21. Ibid., p. 424.

22. Perry Anderson editorial, "Jottings on the Conjuncture," *New Left Review*, November-December 2007, http://www.new leftreview.org/?page=article&view=2695.

23. Horowitz, *Radical Son*, p. 382.

24. *Hitch-22*, p. 139.

25. Ibid., p. 232.

26. Ibid., pp. 232–33.

27. Christopher Hitchens, "Not Even a Hedgehog: The Stupidity of Ronald Reagan," *Slate*, June 7, 2004, http://www.slate.com/id/2101842.

28. Christopher Hitchens, "The Chorus and the Cassandra," in *Grand Street*, Autumn 1985, http://www.chomsky.info/onchomsky/1985----.htm. For a critique of Hitchens' article, see "The Chorus and Cassandra: A Response," *Cambodia*, http://www.mekong.net/cambodia/hitchens.htm.

29. *Hitch-22*, p. 416n.

30. David Horowitz, "A Radical's Disenchantment," *The Nation*, December 8, 1979. Reprinted in *Left Illusions* as the chapter "Left Illusions."

31. *Hitch-22*, p. 268.

32. Horowitz, *Radical Son*, pp. 320–21.

33. *Hitch-22*, p. 333. This was an answer Christopher gave to the "Proust questionnaire."

34. Ibid., p. 87.

35. Video available at http://sciencestage.com/v/32455/why-christopher-hitchens-called-himself-a-trotskyist.html.

36. I have written about Deutscher's misreading of the Russian Revolution in an essay titled, "The Road to Nowhere," which can be found in *The Politics of Bad Faith*, 1998. My commen-

tary on Christopher's review of the Deutscher trilogy can be found here: David Horowitz, "David Horowitz Versus Christopher Hitchens," History News Network, July 30, 2002, http://hnn.us/articles/893.html.

37. Article in *The Atlantic Monthly*, July/August 2004, http://www.theatlantic.com/past/issues/2004/07/hitchens.htm.

38. I am indebted to Peter Collier for this observation.

39. Video available at: http://www.youtube.com/v/K6rRA64f9ug&hl=en&fs=1.

40. *Hitch-22*, p. 5.

41. Again, I am indebted to Peter Collier for this observation.

42. "An Interview with Christopher Hitchens in Simon Cottee and Thomas Cushman, eds. *Christopher Hitchens and His Critics* (New York University Press, 2008), p. 169.

43. *Hitch-22*, p. 139.

44. Ibid.

45. Ibid., p. 138.

46. Ibid., p. 215.

47. Ibid., p. 236.

48. Ibid., p. 237.

49. Ibid.

50. Ibid., p. 238.

51. Cottee and Cushman, eds. *Christopher Hitchens and His Critics*, p. 173.

52. *Hitch-22*, p. 410.

53. Cottee and Cushman, *Christopher Hitchens and His Critics*, p. 173.

54. David Horowitz, "Hats off to a condemned man," *Salon*, March 1, 1999, http://www.salon.com/news/col/horo/1999/03/01/nc_01horo.

55. David Horowitz, *Hating Whitey and Other Progressive Causes* (Spence Publishing, 1999), p. 245 (hereafter *Hating Whitey*). The article first appeared in *Salon.* My *Salon* column was terminated when it became a paid subscription magazine because, its editors explained, their readership wouldn't pay to read the views of a conservative.

56. Horowitz, *Hating Whitey*, pp. 246–47.

57. Cottee and Cushman, *Christopher Hitchens and His Critics.*

58. Interview in Frontpagemag.com, December 10, 2003. Reprinted in Cottee and Cushman, *Christopher Hitchens and His Critics*, p. 173.

59. Cottee and Cushman, *Christopher Hitchens and His Critics*, p. 174.

60. *Hitch-22*, p. 243.

61. Ibid., p. 244.

62. Ibid., p. 245.

63. Ibid., p. 247.

64. Ibid., p. 295.

65. Christopher's review appeared in the November 16, 2003 *Los Angeles Times* and is reprinted in Cottee and Cushman, *Christopher Hitchens and His Critics.* The citation appears on p. 191.

66. *Hitch-22*, p. 411.

67. Ibid., pp. 405–6; Peter Hitchens, *The Broken Compass*, pp. 173, et seq.

68. *Hitch-22*, p. 422.

69. Ibid., p. 394 Emphasis in original.

70. Ibid., p. 376.

71. Ibid., p. 282.

72. Ibid., p. 380.

73. Ibid., p. 382.

74. Ibid., p. 381.

75. Ibid., p. 46.

76. Hitchens, "Topic of Cancer," *Vanity Fair*, article formerly available at: http://www.vanityfair.com/culture/features/2010/09/hitchens-201009.

77. Ibid.

78. Ibid.

79. Christopher Hitchens interviewed by Anderson Cooper. Video available at: http://www.youtube.com/watch?v=LgCq2T-v-Mo.

80. Sonia Verma, "Christopher Hitchens: 'My life is my writing… my children come later,'" *Globe and Mail*, October 22, 2010, http://www.theglobeandmail.com/news/world/christopher-hitchens-my-life-is-my-writing-my-children-come-later/article1769836/singlepage/.

81. Ibid.

82. "Christopher Hitchens on Suffering, Beliefs and Dying," NPR, October 29, 2010, http://www.npr.org/templates/story/story.php?storyId=130917506.

83. Ibid.

84. Ibid.

85. "Tumortown," *Vanity Fair*, http://www.vanityfair.com/culture/features/2010/11/hitchens-201011.

86. Christopher Hitchens, *Arguably: Essays by Christopher Hitchens* (Hachette, 2011).

Chapter Two

1. Bettina Aptheker, *Intimate Politics: How I Grew Up Red, Fought For Free Speech, And Became A Feminist Rebel* (Seal Press, 2006), p. 13.

2. Ibid., p. 1.
3. Ibid., p. 296.
4. Ibid., p. 4. There is, of course, a large literature challenging the very existence of "recovered memory" such as Aptheker claims. Cf. Frederick Crews, "The Revenge of the Repressed," parts I and II in *Follies of the Wise* (Shoemaker & Hoard, 2006), pp. 91 et seq. In composing this portrait, I have suspended judgment on this issue because what is germane is not the truth of the memory but the use to which Bettina Aptheker puts it.
5. Aptheker, *Intimate Politics*, p. 27.
6. Ibid., p. 2.
7. Ibid., p. 527.
8. Ibid.
9. Ibid., pp. 531–32.
10. Ibid., p. 539.
11. Ibid., p. 34
12. Ibid., p. 21. For my recollections of this, cf. *Radical Son* (Touchstone, 1997).
13. Aptheker, *Intimate Politics*, p. 22.
14. Ibid., p. 23.
15. Ibid., p. 384.
16. Ibid., pp. 17–18.
17. Ibid.
18. Ibid., pp. 52–53.
19. Ibid., p. 34.
20. Ibid., p. 27.
21. Ibid., p 28.
22. Ibid., p. 54.
23. Ibid., pp. 20–21.
24. Ibid., p. 27.

25. Ibid., p. 23.
26. I was a childhood friend of several of the families whose fathers "disappeared."
27. Aptheker, *Intimate Politics*, p. 99.
28. Ibid., p. 110.
29. Ibid., p. 107.
30. Ibid., p. 108.
31. Ibid., p. 114.
32. Ibid., p. 115.
33. Ibid., p. 116.
34. Ibid., p. 117.
35. Ibid., p. 118.
36. Ibid.
37. Ibid., p. 119.
38. Ibid.
39. Ibid., p. 128.
40. I have written about these events and Bettina's role in them in *Uncivil Wars: The Controversy Over Reparations for Slavery* (Encounter, 2001).
41. Even Aptheker's account concedes this, Uncivil Wars, op., cit. pp. 126–27, 165.
42. I have documented this transformation in several books, including *The Professors, One-Party Classroom*, and *Reforming Our Universities*.
43. Aptheker, *Intimate Politics*, p. 131.
44. Ibid., p. 174.
45. Ibid., pp. 176 et seq.
46. Ibid., p. 179.
47. Ibid., pp. 193–94.

48. Ibid., p. 207.

49. Ibid., p. 187.

50. Ibid., p. 186.

51. Ibid., p. 55.

52. Ibid., p. 209.

53. Ibid, p. 454.

54. Ibid., pp. 236–37.

55. An account of Jackson's prison career can be found in James Carr, *Bad* (AK Press, 2002). Carr was a member of Jackson's prison gang and the Black Panther Party. When he was released, he served as Huey Newton's bodyguard until he himself was murdered, many suspect by Newton.

56. Gregory Armstrong, *The Dragon Has Come* (Harper & Row, 1974); Jo Durden-Smith, *Who Killed George Jackson?* (Random House, 1976). On Jackson's criminal prison activities—also concealed by Aptheker—see Carr, *Bad*.

57. Aptheker, *Intimate Politics*, p. 245.

58. Ibid., p. 246.

59. Ibid., p. 273.

60. Ibid., p. 248.

61. Ibid., p. 261.

62. Ibid., p. 329.

63. Ibid., p. 283.

64. Ibid., pp. 282–83.

65. Ibid., p. 287.

66. Ibid., p. 297.

67. Ibid., p. 301.

68. Ibid., p. 313.

69. Ibid., p. 337.

70. Ibid.

71. Ibid., p. 345.

72. Ibid.

73. Ibid.

74. Ibid., p. 346.

75. Ibid., p. 347.

76. Ibid., p. 373.

77. Ibid., pp. 347–48.

78. Ibid., p. 350.

79. Bettina Aptheker, *Women's Legacy: Essays on Race, Sex, and Class* (University of Massachusetts Press, 1982), pp. 133–34.

80. Aptheker, *Intimate Politics*, pp. 351–52.

81. Ibid., p. 392.

82. Ibid.

83. Ibid., p. 403.

84. Ibid.

85. Ibid., p. 406.

86. Ibid., p. 437.

87. Ibid., p. 408.

88. Ibid., p. 404.

89. Ibid., p. 405.

90. Ibid., p. 406.

91. Ibid., p. 473.

92. Ibid., p. 438.

93. Ibid., p.480.

94. Ibid., pp. 500–1.

95. Ibid., p. 525.

96. Ibid., p. 505.

97. Ibid., p. 495.
98. Ibid., p. 498.

Chapter Three

1. Aaron Klein with Brenda J. Elliott, *The Manchurian President* (WND Books, 2010), p.101.
2. Cornel West, *Brother West: Living and Loving Out Loud* (Smiley Books, 2009), p. 227.
3. Ibid.
4. Ibid., flap copy.
5. Ibid.
6. Sam Tanenhaus, "Right-Wing Blacklist," *Slate*, June 20, 2002 http://www.slate.com/articles/arts/culturebox/2002/06/rightwing_blacklist.html.
7. West, *Brother West*, p. 250.
8. Ibid., pp. 247–48.
9. Ibid., pp. 249–50.
10. Ibid., p. 5.
11. Global March to Jerusalem, http://gm2j.com/main/north american-personalities/.
12. Cornel West, *Hope on a Tightrope: Words and Wisdom*, 2008 (Kindle Edition), loc. 1350–60.
13. The $35,000 fee was divulged to me by the president of the University of Denver, the institution that provided it.
14. West, *Brother West*, p. 185.
15. West, *Hope on a Tightrope*, pp. 262–67.
16. Ibid., pp. 607–12.
17. Ibid., pp. 406–12.

18. Readings and Conversations, Cornel West, June 25, 2003, the Lannan Foundation, www.lannan.org/images/cf/cornel-west-030625-trans-read.pdf.

19. West, *Brother West*, p. 22.

20. Ibid., p. 103.

21. James Cone profile, DiscovertheNetworks.org, http://www.discoverthenetworks.org/individualProfile.asp?indid=2315.

22. West, *Brother West*, p. 70.

23. Amiri Baraka profile, DiscovertheNetworks.org, http://www.discoverthenetworks.org/individualProfile.asp?indid=2171.

24. West, *Brother West*, p. 70.

25. Amiri Baraka profile, op cit.

26. West, *Brother West*, p. 67.

27. Elijah Muhammad profile, DiscovertheNetworks.org, http://www.discoverthenetworks.org/individualProfile.asp?indid=1581.

28. West, *Brother West*, pp. 68–70.

29. Ibid.

30. Ibid., p. 68.

31. Ibid., p. 69.

32. Ibid., pp. 69–70.

33. Ibid., p. 23.

34. Louis Farrakhan profile, DiscovertheNetworks.org, http://www.discoverthenetworks.org/individualProfile.asp?indid=1325.

35. David Horowitz, *The Politics of Bad Faith* (Free Press, 1998).

36. Bob Avakian, *From Ike to Mao and Beyond* (Insight Press, 2005).

37. Al Sharpton profile, DiscovertheNetworks.org, http://www.discoverthenetworks.org/individualProfile.asp?indid=1527.

38. Louis Farrakhan profile, op. cit.

39. Michael Lerner and Cornel West, *Jews & Blacks: Let the Healing Begin* (Putnam Adult, 1995), p. 249.

40. Ibid.

41. Leon Wieseltier, "The Unreal World of Cornel West," *New Republic*, March 6, 1995.

42. Michael Lerner profile, DiscovertheNetworks, http://www. discoverthenetworks.org/individualProfile.asp?indid=632. Lerner's full network is available here: http://www.discover thenetworks.org/search/?cx=013255222075609514560%3Avfc ebs4vcuo&q=michael+lerner&sa=Search&cof=FORID%3A1 1&cx=013255222075609514560%3Avfcebs4vcuo&siteurl= www.discoverthenetworks.org%2Fsearch%2F#987

43. Hamas profile, DiscovertheNetworks.org, http://www.discover thenetworks.org/groupProfile.asp?grpid=6204.

44. Lerner and West, *Jews & Blacks*.

45. West, *Brother West*, p. 187.

46. Ibid.

47. West, *Brother West*, pp. 187–88.

48. Lerner and West, *Jews & Blacks*, p. 6.

49. Ibid.

50. Leon Wieseltier, "The Unreal World of Cornel West."

51. Ibid.

52. West, *Brother West*, p. 189.

53. Andrew Delbanco, "SKIRMISHES; The Decline of Discourse," *New York Times*, April 16, 1993, http://www.nytimes. com/1995/04/16/books/skirmishes-the-decline-of-discourse. html?pagewanted=all.

54. West, *Brother West*, pp. 218–19.

55. Ibid., p. 218.

56. Ibid.

57. Ibid., p. 219.

58. Ibid., pp. 219–20.

59. Ibid., p. 228.

60. Fact Sheets, "#12: The Anti-Semitic Divestment Campaign," Jewish Virtual Library, February 9, 2006, http://www.jewish virtuallibrary.org/jsource/talking/12_Divest.html.

61. Zachary Seward, "Summers's supporters withhold $390 million from Harvard," *Wall Street Journal*, published in the *Pittsburgh Post-Gazette*, March 16, 2012, http://www.post-gazette.com/pg/06194/705613-28.stm.

62. Cornel West, *Democracy Matters* (Penguin, 2004), p. 41.

63. Ibid., p. 22.

64. Ibid., p. 4.

65. Ibid., p. 6.

66. Ibid., p. 8.

Chapter Four

1. Information previously available here: http://archive.prison activist.org/prisoners/linda-evans. Currently available at DiscoverTheNetworks.org, http://www.discoverthenetworks.org/funderprofile.asp?fndid=5362&category=79.

2. Linda Sue Evans bio, http://en.wikipedia.org/wiki/Linda_Evans_%28radical%29.

3. Alex Altman, "Sarah Jane Olson: American Housewife, American Terrorist, *Time*, March 18, 2009, http://www.time.com/time/nation/article/0,8599,1885965,00.html.

4. Jamil Abdullah Al-Amin (a.k.a. Rap Brown) profile, DiscovertheNetworks.org, http://www.discoverthenetworks.org/individualProfile.asp?indid=1308.

5. Robert Worth, "Lines Are Drawn as 60's Radical Seeks Parole for an 80's Crime," *New York Times*, August 20, 2001, http://www.nytimes.com/2001/08/20/nyregion/lines-are-drawn-as-60-s-radical-seeks-parole-for-an-80-s-crime.html?pagewanted=all&src=pm.

6. Susan Braudy, *Family Circle: The Boudins and the Aristocracy of the Left* (Knopf/Doubleday, 2004), p. 380.

7. Ibid., p. 370.

8. Ibid.

9. This story has been ably told in John Castellucci, *The Big Dance: The Untold Story of Kathy Boudin and the Terrorist Family that Committed the Brinks' Robbery Murders* (Dodd, Mead, 1986).

10. Braudy, *Family Circle*, pp. 300–1.

11. Ibid., p. 285.

12. Ibid., pp. 381–84 http://www.google.com/search?q=kathy+boudin+parole+hearing+transcript&ie=utf-8&oe=utf-8&aq=t&rls=org.mozilla:en-US:official&client=firefox-a.

13. James C. McKinley Jr., "Parole Officials Won't Appeal Decision to Free Kathy Boudin," *New York Times*, August 23, 2003, http://www.nytimes.com/2003/08/23/nyregion/parole-officials-won-t-appeal-decision-to-free-kathy-boudin.html?src=pm.

14. Braudy, *Family Circle*, pp. 139–42.

15. I have edited this email and also my replies only as necessary to protect Rachel's identity and to keep the promise I made to her.

16. For a lengthy, informed review of Rosenberg's book, see George Russell, "The Other Rosenberg Case," *Commentary* magazine, May 2011, http://www.commentarymagazine.com/article/the-other-rosenberg-case/.

17. Braudy, *Family Circle*, pp. 364–65; "An American Radical: A Conversation with Susan Rosenberg," KPCC, April 16, 2011

event description, http://www.scpr.org/events/2011/04/16/american-radical-conversation-susan-rosenberg/.

18.   Tom Robbins, "Judith Clark's Radical Transformation," *New York Times*, January 12, 2012, http://www.nytimes.com/2012/01/15/magazine/judith-clarks-radical-transformation.html?_r=2.

Chapter Six

1.   Richard Rorty, *Achieving Our Country: Leftist Thought in Twentieth-Century America* (Harvard University Press, 1998). This aphorism was used as an epigraph in Michael Kazin's history of American leftism, aptly titled *American Dreamers: How the Left Changed a Nation* (Knopf, 2011). Kazin's history is about the ideals he imagines leftists have contributed to America's heritage, not the actual actions leftists have conducted in the political arena.

2.   Saul Alinsky, *Rules for Radicals*, p. xiii.

3.   Sanford Horwitt, *Let Them Call Me Rebel* (Vintage Books, 1992), p. 20.

4.   Alinsky, *Reveille for Radicals* (Vintage edition, 1969), p. 227.

5.   See video of this speech at http://www.youtube.com/watch?v=molWTfv8TYw.

6.   Alinsky, *Rules for Radicals*.

7.   Bill Dedman, "Reading Hillary Rodham's hidden thesis," MSNBC, May 9, 2007, http://www.msnbc.msn.com/id/17388372/.

8.   The statement appeared in *New Left Notes*.

9.   Ryan Lizza, "The Agitator," *New Republic*, March 19, 2007. See http://www.tnr.com/article/the-agitator. The source of the anecdote is Horwitt, *Let Them Call Me Rebel*.

10. Alinsky, *Rules for Radicals*, p. 113.

11. Peter Slevin, "For Clinton and Obama, a Common Ideological Touchstone," *Washington Post*, March 25, 2007, http://www.washingtonpost.com/wp-dyn/content/article/2007/03/24/AR2007032401152_pf.html.

12. David Freddoso, *The Case Against Barack Obama* (Regnery, 2008). Cited in DiscoverTheNetworks' profile of Barack Obama, http://www.discoverthenetworks.org/individualProfile.asp?indid=1511.

13. Ryan Lizza, "The Agitator."

14. Barack Hussein Obama profile, DiscoverTheNetworks, http://www.discoverthenetworks.org/individualProfile.asp?indid=1511.

15. Ibid.

16. Ibid.

17. Slevin, "For Clinton and Obama, a Common Ideological Touchstone."

18. John Fund, "Acorn Who?" *Wall Street Journal*, September 21, 2009, http://online.wsj.com/article/SB10001424052970204488304574427041636360388.html#.

19. Lizza, "The Agitator."

20. Alinsky, *Rules for Radicals*, p. xiii.

21. Ibid., p. xix.

22. Transcript, "Michelle Obama's Remarks at the Democratic Convention," *New York Times*, August 26, 2008, http://www.nytimes.com/2008/08/26/us/politics/26text-obama.html?ei=5124&en=48bdd187be31e21e&ex=1377489600&partner=permalink&exprod=permalink&pagewanted=print.

23. Eliza Strickland, "The New Face of Environmentalism," *East Bay Express*, November 2, 2005, http://www.eastbayexpress.com/

gyrobase/the_new_face_of_environmentalism/Content?oid=2
90098&showFullText=true.

24. Alinsky, *Rules for Radicals*, p. xviii.

25. Ibid., p. 37.

26. Ibid., p. 3.

27. Ibid., p. 18.

28. Ibid., p. 7.

29. "Indoctrination Studies," DiscoverTheNetworks.com, http://
www.discoverthenetworks.org/viewSubCategory.
asp?id=522#Curricular_Studies.

30. See video of this speech at http://www.youtube.com/
watch?v=KrefKCaV8m4; cf. Stanley Kurtz, *Radical-in-Chief*
(Threshold Editions, 2010) for a well documented account of
Obama's leftist career.

31. The Nixon administration was then negotiating with the North
Vietnamese Communists to arrive at a peace agreement.

32. Not very likely.

33. Horwitt, *Let Them Call Me Rebel*, pp. xv–xvi.

34. Alinsky, *Rules for Radicals*, pp. 10–11.

35. Alinsky, *Reveille for Radicals*, p. 21.

36. The comment was made to the author personally.

37. Eric J. Hobsbawm, *Primitive Rebels*, p. 5 Google edition.

38. Ibid., p. 7.

39. Alinsky, *Rules for Radicals*, p. 24.

40. Ibid., p. 29.

41. Leon Trotsky, "Their Morals and Ours," from *The New International*, Vol. IV, No. 6, June 1938, pp. 163–73; available online at:

http://www.marxists.org/archive/trotsky/1938/morals/morals.
htm.

42. Alinsky, *Rules for Radicals*, p. 25.

43. Ibid.

Index

18th Brumaire, The, 182

1992 Democratic Senate primary, 181

9/11, 9, 19, 23, 27, 36, 39, 100, 108, 129, 176

A

ACORN, 180–82

Addison, Joseph, 103

Afghanistan, 36, 125

Africa, 101

African-Americans, 113, 141, 147, 153–54

AIDS, 136, 141, 160

Al-Amin, Jamil Abdullah, 131–34

Alexander, Franklin, 82

Alinsky, Saul, 171–98

  Barack Obama and, 2, 176, 179–81, 184–85

  Cesar Chavez and, 176–77

  communism and, 174

  as community organizer, 173

  Democratic Party and, 172, 176–77

  Hillary Clinton and, 177, 179

  liberals and, 193, 195

  lying as tactic of, 183, 186

  power and, 178

  progressives and, 5

  revolution and, 175

  Satan and, 182–83, 194

Vladimir Lenin and, 185, 192, 197–98

Althusser, Louis, 114

Alvarez, A. A., 14

America
as "Amerikkka," 128, 153
as imperialist, 18, 30, 97, 122
as oppressor, 18, 30, 40, 123–26, 131, 144, 151, 173
as racist, 30, 122–23, 125,1 44, 151
as unjust, 30, 151, 173

American Communists, 183

American Founders, 186

American Muslim Council, 133

American Negro Slave Revolts, 58, 81

American Radical: How I Was a Political Prisoner in My Own Country, An, 126, 143, 144, 147, 172

Amis, Martin, 13, 27, 46

Anderson, Perry, 19

Angelou, Maya, 83, 10

anti-globalization movement, 176

anti-Iraq War movement, 37, 176

anti-semitism, 115–18

Apollo Alliance, 184

Aptheker, Bettina, 2, 57–97
arrests of, 74, 84
Buddhism and, 93–95, 97
childhood of, 62–67
children of, 65, 74–76
Communist Party and, 90–91

family of, 57–59, 65
as feminist, 88–89, 92
as lesbian, 84, 93
marriage of, 85
memoir of, 60, 84
sexual abuse of, 60–61
university career of, 87–88, 92
as victim, 60, 66, 69–71, 77, 81

Aptheker, Fay, 60, 64, 79

Aptheker, Herbert, 57, 59, 60, 63, 67, 69, 91, 94, 97

Aptheker, Joshua, 75, 77

Arab Spring, 50

Arica, 161–62, 165

Asquith, 29

Associated Press, 156

Atlanta, 49, 133–34

Atlanta Community Mosque, 133

Atlantic Monthly, 25

Avakian, Bob ("Chairman Bob"), 114

Ayers, Bill, 128, 136, 172, 191

B

Balliol College, 15

Baraka, Imamu Amiri, 107–9, 115

barbarism, 29

Barnard College, 138

Bay Area Communist, 92

Benjamin, Walter, 59

Berkeley, 7, 57–59, 68, 69, 71–76, 92, 127–28, 165, 169

Berlin Wall, 21–22, 26, 95

Beverly Hills, 46

"Big Brother and the Holding Company," 161

Bird, Kai, 8

Black Liberation Army, 135–39, 145, 149–50

Black Panthers, 23, 82

Black Student Association, 107

black theology, 107, 114

Black Theology and Marxist Thought, 114

Blackburn, Robin, 19

Blair, Tony, 49

Blumenthal, Sidney, 32–33

Bolsheviks, 16–17, **24**, 26, 67, 185

Bonnie and Clyde, 194

"Book Notes," 20

Book of Job, 186

Bosnia, 23, 35

Boston Globe, 124

Boudin, Chesa, 136

Boudin, Kathy, 2, 131, 135–41, 152–53

Bouey, Daizzee, 141

Bradley, Bill, 99, 117, 120

Braudy, Susan, 136

Braun, Carol Moseley, 181

Brinks robbery, 136, 138, 145, 150, 152

Brooklyn, 74, 115

Brother West: Living and Loving Out Loud, 103

Brown, H. Rap, 133

Brown, Waverly, 136–38, 145

Bryn Mawr, 135

Buddhism, 94

Bush administration, 130

Bush, George H. W., 96, 191–93

Bush, George W., 37

C

California, 57, 68, 85, 87, 127

Cambodia, 18, 19, 22

Capitol building, 128–29

Capone, Al, 173, 194

Carmichael, Stokely, 115

Carter, Jimmy, 145

Carthage, 198

Castro, Fidel, 19, 30, 33, 37, 197

Castroism, 30

Catholic Church, 26

Catholic pope, 49

CBS, 152

Central America, 129

Chapman, Shawn, 132–33

Chavez, Cesar, 176–77

Chesimard, Joanne, 139, 149–50

Chez Panisse, 169

Children's Defense Fund, 101

Chomsky, Noam, 22–23, 31, 36, 40, 139

Christianity, 40–41

Christians, 39, 104, 124, 183

Churchill, Winston, 29

CIO, 174

Civil Rights Acts, 141

civil rights movement, 18, 112, 141 *see also* African-Americans

Clark, Judith, 153

Cleaver, Eldridge, 147

Clifford, Jim, 87

Clinton administration, 100, 185

Clinton, Bill, 31, 99, 127

Clinton, Hillary Rodham, 101, 177, 179

Close, Glenn, 137

Cockburn, Alex, 8, 32–33

Cold War, 37, 50, 58, 113, 174, 175

Coleman, Kate, 151

Collier, Peter, 8, 13, 17, 20, 21, 23, 155

Columbia University, 100, 181, 191

Columbus, Christopher, 36

communism, 3, 21, 26, 64, 113, 114, 118, 173, 174

Communist guerrilla armies, 129

Communist Manifesto, 187–88

Communist Party, 57, 68, 71, 75, 80, 82, 84, 85, 90, 91, 114, 173

community organizing, 181

Cone, James, 107, 109

conservative principles, 171

Cooper, Anderson, 47

Cornel West Academy of Excellence, 101

Cuba, 79, 139, 148

D

Daily Kos, 191

Dalai Lama, 57, 93–94

Dallas News, 156

Davis, Angela, 78–84, 87–88, 134, 148, 191

Days of Rage, 129

de Beauvoir, Simon, 46

Debs, Eugene, 177

democracy, 3, 31, 42–43, 96, 102, 106, 118, 125, 147, 175, 177, 179, 181, 186, 188–89

Democracy Matters, 102, 124

Democratic Party, 99, 172, 176–77, 183, 185

Democratic Socialists of America, 113

Department of Feminist Studies, 93

Destructive Generation, 4, 20

Deutscher, Isaac, 25–26

Die Welt, 156

Dillinger, John, 194

Dixon, Alan, 181

dogmatism, 174

Dohrn, Bernardine, 128, 136, 191, 194

Dostoevsky, Fyodor, 197

DuBois Club, 71

DuBois, W. E. B., 58, 91

Durkheim, Emile, 14

E

Eagleton, Terry, 11

East Germany, 76, 95

Eastern Europe, 22, 118, 174

Edelman, Marian Wright, 101

England, 15, 47, 158

Enron, 188

Ensler, Eve, 137

Epstein, Barbara, 92

Europe, 35, 106, 166

Evans, Linda, 127–35, 138–40, 153

evil, 3, 28, 40, 180, 187, 189, 192, 194, 197

Ezekiel, 100

F

Family, The, 137–39, 153

Farrakhan, Louis, 110, 112–13, 115–17

fascism, 21, 35, 43, 51, 58, 67, 185

FBI, 31, 63, 70, 72, 74, 77, 80–81, 129

feminism, 4, 9, 57–97, 119, 123, 157–58

"feminist rebel," 71

Ferragamo, 168

Fetchit, Stepin, 126

Firestone, Shulamith, 86

Fisherman's Wharf, 155

Fonda, Jane, 18

Forbes, Jim, 107

Forster, E. M., 167

Fort Dix, 128, 140

"Free Angela Davis Committee," 71–72, 74, 76, 81

Free Speech Movement

Freud, Sigmund, 104, 158

    theory of feminine sexuality of, 158

From Ike to Mao and Beyond, 114

FrontPageMag.com, 5

fundamentalism, 22, 125

G

Galluzzo, Gregory, 180

Gamaliel Foundation, 180

Gates of Eden, 198

Gaza, 42–43, 117

George X, 109–11

German Ideology, 190

Germany, 29, 64, 76, 95, 101, 190, 194

Gilbert, David, 138

Gitlin, Todd, 33

Giuliani, Rudy, 139, 150

"Global March to Jerusalem," 104

God, 10, 27, 29, 46, 49, 93, 104–5, 109, 111, 125, 182–83, 197–98

God Is Not Great: How Religion Poisons Everything, 29, 39, 44

Goethe, Johann Wolfgang, 182

Gold, Ted, 127–28, 137

Goldenbergs, the, 166

Good and Evil, 187

Gramsci, Antonio, 114

Greenwich Village, 128

Guevara, Che, 146

Guggenheim Foundation, 108

Gulf War, 96

H

Hamas, 9, 51, 53

Harlem, 99, 115, 139

Harvard University, 99–101, 104, 107–9, 112, 117, 119–24

Have-a-Little, Want Mores, 187

Have-nots, 186–89, 191, 196

Haves, 175, 178, 186–91, 196

Hayden, Tom, 176, 194

Healy, Dorothy, 33

Hearst, Patty, 132–33

Hernandez, Raul, 68–69

Hezbollah, 51

Hinduism , 39

Hiss, Alger, 9, 19, 53

history, 15, 18, 24–26, 28–29, 41, 55, 61, 64, 75, 89, 113, 125, 168, 175, 182, 187–89, 198

"History of Black Women," 84

"History of Consciousness," 87, 91

Hitch-22, 9, 12, 23, 29, 37
    "A *Coda* on the Question of Self-Slaughter" chapter, 14
    "Topic of Cancer" chapter, 45

Hitchens, Carol, 13

Hitchens, Christopher, 2, 4, 7–55
    9/11 and, 9, 19, 23, 36, 39
    atheism of, 40, 44
    cancer of, 44–45, 54–55
    children of, 13, 45, 48
    death of, 45, 48–50, 54–55
    marriages of, 13
    mother of, 14–15
    second thoughts and, 4, 17, 37, 43, 48, 52

    as "Snitchens," 33

Hitchens, Peter, 16–18, 24, 39

Hitchens, Yvonne, 10, 13–15, 27, 40, 42, 47, 50

Hitler, Adolf, 186

Ho Chi Minh, 18, 139

Hobsbawm, Eric, 59, 114, 134, 195

Hoffman, Abbie, 176, 194

holocaust
    Cambodian, 22
    Jewish, 22, 115

Homer, 10

Hope on a Tightrope: Words and Wisdom, 105

Horwitt, Sanford, 191

House Judiciary Committee, 129

Howard University, 117

Howards End, 167

Howe, Irving, 59

Hungary, 58, 72, 76

Hussein, Saddam, 36–37, 96

I

Ichazo, Oscar, 161

idealism, 5, 140, 152, 154, 160, 172, 175, 178, 180–81, 183, 193–94

"identity politics," 59, 95

Illinois Senate, 182

imperialism, 51, 114, 124, 131, 136

Industrial Areas Foundation (IAF), 175, 179–80

Interesting Times, 59

International Publishers, 83, 88

International Socialists, 16–18, 51

Intimate Politics: How I Grew Up Red, Fought for Free Speech, and Became a Feminist Rebel, 58–59, 62

"A Wedding, A Trial, and A War" chapter, 74

"Introduction to Feminism" course, 92

Iraq, 9, 19, 29, 36–37, 39, 106, 125, 176

Iraq War, 9, 19, 37, 39

Islamic jihadists, 34–35, 40, 100, 125, 127

Islamo-fascism, 43

Israel, 8, 19, 42–43, 116–17, 122–23, 125, 129

Israeli Aircraft Industries, 129

J

Jackson, George, 23, 57, 78–80, 82–83, 147

Jackson, Jesse, 33, 115, 177

Jackson, Jonathan, 79–83, 147–49

James, Henry, 127

Janus, 10

Jaures, Jean, 29

Jeffersonian Democrats, 183

Jesus Christ, 61, 105, 107, 113, 117, 195

Jews, 10, 15, 22, 39–43, 51, 104–5, 107–8, 115–18, 123–24, 126, 174

Jews and Blacks: Let the Healing Begin, 117

jihad, 34–35, 39–40, 100, 125, 127

Johnson, Lyndon B., 18, 89, 176

Johnson, Paul, 8–9

Johnson, Virginia E., 158

Jones, LeRoi *see* Baraka, Imamu Amiri

Jones, Serene, 99

Jones, Van, 184–85

Jong-Il, Kim, 37

Joplin, Janis, 161

Judaism, 40–42

"Judith Clark's Radical Transformation," 153

K

Karamazov, Ivan, 155

Kennedy, John F., 18

Kennedy, Robert, 177

KGB, 31

Khomeini, Ayatollah, 23, 35

King Jr., Martin Luther, 112, 147, 177

Kinsey, Alfred, 158

Kirkland, Martha, 74

Kirkpatrick, Jeane, 35

Kissinger, Henry, 35

Klinkner, Phil, 151

Knitting Heaven and Earth, 167

Knitting Sutra: Craft as a Spiritual Practice, The, 166

Kodak, 177

Kremlin, the, 72

Kronstadt revolt, 24

Ku Klux Klan, 192

Kunstler, William, 139

Kurzweil, Jack, 68, 73, 85

Kuwait, 96

L

Laksell, John, 3, 5

Lannan Foundation, 106

Lapham, Lewis, 20

Lebanon, 8, 51

left, the, 7–9, 16, 20, 30–36, 38, 59, 74,
 79–80, 84, 119, 126, 140, 151–52,
 158, 174, 187

Left Illusions, 4, 37

Lehman, 188

Lenin, Vladimir, 90, 175, 179, 185–86,
 192–93, 197–98

Lerner, Michael, 116–18

Let Them Call Me Rebel, 191

Lewis, John L., 174

Liebknecht, Karl, 29

Lima, Mickey, 68

Lizza, Ryan, 180

London, 18, 156–57

London *Guardian*, 156–59

London *Telegraph*, 156

Los Angeles Times, 34, 156–57

Lucifer *see also* Satan, 182–83, 194

Lukacs, Gyorgy, 114

Luxemburg, Rosa, 24, 29

Lydon, Michael, 156

Lydon, Shuna, 156, 161, 163–64, 169

Lydon, Susan, 155–68

M

Machiavelli, Niccolo, 171–98

Machiavellians, 178, 185

Malcolm X, 107, 109–10, 112–13, 139

Manicheans, 188–89

Mansfield, Harvey, 120

Manson, Charles, 194

Mao Tse-Tung's Immortal Contribution,
 114

Mao Zedong, 114, 185

Maoism, 33, 114, 184

Marcuse, Herbert, 59

Marin County, 79, 83, 148

marriage, 13, 59, 73, 85, 95, 160

Martin, Evelyn, 68–69, 71

Martin, Max, *see also* Mickey Lima,
 68–69, 71, 82

Marx, Karl, 9, 26–28, 87, 89, 118, 172,
 182, 187–90, 197–98

Marxism, 2–3, 11–12, 16, 19, 21, 25,
 27–29, 37, 41, 43, 57, 59, 63, 77, 82,
 86–90, 92, 96, 108, 114, 118–19,
 123, 125, 172, 174, 178, 196

Masters, William H., 158

May 19 Communist Organization, 135,
 137, 144

McCarthy era, 66–67, 174

McCarthy, Joseph, 31

McCarthyism, 33, 66–67, 72

Mephistopheles, 182

Merleau-Ponty, Maurice, 59

Middle East, 8, 43, 51

Midnight Special bookstore, 130, 135, 140

Millay, Edna St. Vincent, 44

Miller, Kate, 63, 93

"Million Man March," 115

Milosevic, Slobodan, 37

Mitchell, Juliet, 86

Mitford, Jessica, 23–24

monogamy, 160

Moore, Michael, 191

Morrison, Toni, 83, 118

Moses, 195

Motor Voter Law, 181

MoveOn.org, 191

Moynihan, Daniel Patrick, 89

Muhammad, Elijah, 109–12

Muslims, 23, 35, 40, 42–43, 111, 133

N

Nadler, Jerrold, 129–30, 140

Napa Valley, 166

Nation magazine, 8, 19, 24, 30–34, 36, 53, 137, 151

Nation of Islam, 109–12, 117

"National Commission on Women," 90

National Committee, 75

National Education Association, 190

National Guardian, 81

National Liberation Front, 17

National War College, 129

NationalReviewOnline.com, 5

Navasky, Victor, 8–9, 19, 31, 53

Navy Yard Computer Center, 129

Navy Yard Officers Club, 129

Nazism, 10, 29, 194

"Nechaevists," 5

"Negro Question," 58

Negroes with Guns, 147

"New Left," 17, 19, 71–72, 75, 80, 82, 86, 183

New Republic, 116, 118, 178, 180

New Statesman, 11

New York Patrolman's Benevolent Association, 129

New York Times, 23, 100, 124, 135, 137, 152, 156

New York Times Book Review, 101

New Yorker, 152

Newsweek, 101, 156

Newton, Huey, 79, 87

Nietzsche, 194

Nitti, Frank, 173, 194

Nixon administration, 192

Nixon, Richard, 192

No One Left to Lie to: The Worst Family, 31

North Vietnamese, 21, 192

Nouvel Observateur, 156

nuclear family, 160

Nyack police force, 137, 145

O

O'Grady, Peter, 138

Oakland Tribune, 156

Obama, Barack, 99–100, 103, 144, 171–72, 176, 178–82, 184–85, 194

Obama, Michelle, 182, 184

Old Left, 183

"old leftists," 82

Olson, Sara Jane, 131–33

Orwell, George, 19, 22

Oval Office, 2

Oxford University, 7, 11, 15, 31

P

P.E.N., 152

Paine, Thomas, 24

Palestine, 8, 42–43, 51, 105, 116–17, 122

patriarchal oppressions, 160

Patriot Act, 125

Pell, Eve, 24

PEN/Faulkner Award, 108

Pentagon, 35, 128, 176

Petrograd, 185

Plath, Sylvia, 14

Podesta, John, 185

Poet Laureate, 108

Point in Time, A, 4

political correctness, 86, 157

political prisoners, 81, 129–30, 140

political sentimentalist, 158

Politics of Bad Faith, The, 4

"Politics of the Orgasm, The," 155

Port Huron, 72

power, 15, 21, 24–25, 27, 33, 35, 66, 73, 86, 93, 95–96, 167, 169, 175, 177–81, 185–87, 191

Prague, 50

Pravda, 23

Primitive Rebels, 195

   "Social Bandits" chapter, 195

Prince, The, 186

Princeton, 99–101, 112, 122–23

prison-industrial complex, 134

progressivism, 1–5, 20, 23–24, 31–33, 39, 60–62, 72, 85, 105, 108, 113, 116, 118–19, 122–26, 129, 132, 139, 141, 143, 158, 171–72, 174–75, 183, 186

Project Vote, 181

Prophet Armed, The, 25

Prophet Outcast, The, 25

Prophet Unarmed, The, 25

Prophetic Fragments, 100

Proudhon, Pierre-Joseph, 195

Pulitzer Prize, 101

Puritan faith, 189

puritanism, 63, 111

Putnam, Hilary, 101

Q

quivit shawl, 167–68

R

race, 86, 88, 104, 107, 109, 118, 121, 128, 183–84, 192

"Rachel," 141–43, 151

racism, 78, 113–14, 128–29, 131, 194

Radical Ruptures, 114

Radical Son, 4

radicalism, 3, 79, 95, 126

Raleigh, North Carolina, 101

Ramparts magazine, 7, 155, 157–61, 164

Reagan, Ronald, 8, 21–22

Reason magazine, 27, 33

Rector, Ricky Ray, 31

Red Army, 21, 24, 174

Renaissance Faires, 127

Reuther, Walter, 174

Reveille for Radicals, 173, 177, 193

Revolution Betrayed, The, 25

Revolutionary Communist Party, 114

revolutionary spirit, 26, 162

Rieff, David, 20–21

rights, 30, 42, 43, 62, 134–35, 137, 141, 145, 147–48, 152, 173, 177, 194, 196

Rockefeller, David, 123

Rockefeller Foundation, 108

Rolling Stone, 157

Rorty, Richard, 172

Rosenbaum, Yankel, 115

Rosenberg, Susan, 2, 138–53

Rosenbergs, the (Julius and Ethel), 9, 53, 62, 66, 81

Rousseau, Jean-Jacques, 197

Rules for Radicals, 174, 178, 182, 186
    as *Rules for Revolution*, 173
    "The Purpose" chapter, 186

Rushdie, Salman, 23, 35, 39, 152

Russia, 5, 16, 23, 49, 175, 195, 197

Russian River, 167

Rutgers University, 108

S

Said, Edward, 40, 101

Salon, 34

San Francisco Chronicle, 156

San Jose State University, 83–84

San Quentin, 68, 79, 82

Satan *see also* Lucifer, 115, 182, 189

Savio, Mario, 72

Scheer, Robert, 159–60

Scipio Africanus, 198

SDS, 72, 127–28, 177, 194

"Seattle Liberation Front," 116

second thoughts, 4, 8–9, 17, 20, 21, 37, 38, 43, 48, 52, 81, 143, 145, 160

Second Thoughts Conference, 8, 20

"Sex and Power" course, 86

sexism, 86, 89, 104, 123, 194

Shakespeare, William, 166

Shakur, Assata *see* Chesimard, Joanne

Sharon, Ariel, 122

Sharpton, Al, 99, 115, 120, 177

Sixties, 2, 31, 79, 84, 109, 116, 131, 133, 160, 175–76, 183, 185, 194

Sketches of My Culture, 121

Smith Act, 67

social class, 7, 15, 28, 41, 64, 86, 88–89, 91–92, 95, 105, 138–39, 186–88, 190, 194, 196

social institutions, 15, 26, 28, 40, 109, 120, 122, 124, 165, 175–76, 178

social justice, 15, 62, 68, 86, 95, 137, 150, 152–53, 171, 176, 178, 183, 186, 191, 195, 197

socialism, 16, 27–29, 62, 95, 172, 186, 195

socialists, 2, 16–17, 28–29

Socrates, 24, 113, 124

Soledad Brother, 79

Soledad Brothers, 79, 147

Soliah, Kathy *see* Olson, Sara Jane

"Somebody Blew Up America," 108

Sontag, Susan, 20–21, 152

Soul on Ice, 147

South Vietnam, 18, 192

Soviet Union, 16–19, 21–22, 26, 30–31, 58, 62, 66–67, 72, 76, 91, 97, 118, 173–74

Spinoza, 24

Stalin, 17, 25, 29, 31, 76

Stalinism, 16, 25, 29, 33, 58, 65

Stanford University, 87

Steal This Book, 194

Steinem, Gloria, 33

Stender, Fay, 79

STORM, 184

Summers, Larry, 100, 104, 120–23

Symbionese Liberation Army, 132–33

T

Take the Long Way Home, 160, 165

Tannenhaus, Sam, 101

terrorism, 2, 5, 8, 80, 106, 122, 125, 129, 135, 137, 141

Their Morals and Ours, 195

"There Is Only the Fight: An Analysis of the Alinsky Model," 177

Theresa, 167–68

Third Reich, 22

"Three Essays on The Theory of Sexuality," 158

Tijuana, 69

Tikkun, 116

Time, 101, 121

Timothy, Mary, 83–85

Tree of Knowledge, 182

Trilling, Lionel, 3

Trotsky, Leon, 7, 9, 16–17, 19, 24–27, 31, 195–96

Truth about Hungary, The, 58

Tuck, 160–61

Tulane University, 191

Ture, Kwame *see* Carmichael, Stokely

Turkey, 42, 117
Turner, Nat, 58, 61

U

Ulysses, 10
United Nations, 191
Unholy Alliance, 4
Union Theological Seminary, 99
United Farmworkers, 176
"United Front," 71
United States, 8, 18, 34–35, 40, 97, 171,
     180, 191–92
University of California Berkeley, 7,
     57–59, 68–69, 71, 73–76, 81, 92,
     127–28, 160, 165, 169
University of California, Santa Cruz,
     87, 92, 96
University of Chicago, 173
University of Paris, 100
"University Professors," 100, 119–20
utopia, 1, 5, 28, 38–40, 43–44, 51, 95,
     172, 193–94, 197
Uzi, 139

V

Vagina Monologues, The, 137
Van Patter, Betty, 151
Vanity Fair, 36, 44–45
Vassar, 161
Victorian era, 158
Victorian society, 158

Victorian women, 158
Vidal, George, 31
Vietcong, 30, 116
Vietnam, 9, 17–19, 21, 31, 74–75, 83,
     128, 145, 191–92
Vietnam War, 31, 145, 191–92
Village Voice, 119
Voltaire, 40

W

Walden School, 138
Wall Street Journal, 181
Washington, D.C., 32, 74, 112, 115, 128
Washington, Jim, 107
Washington Post, 179
Weather Underground, 128, 130, 135,
     137–38, 153
Weatherman, 127–29, 172, 194
Weir, David, 151
Wellesley, 177, 179
West Bank, 42–43, 117
West, Cornel, 3, 5, 99–126
West Side Story, 68
White, Hayden, 87, 91w
White House, 18, 22, 31–32, 99–100,
     119, 129, 144, 176, 179, 185
White House Council of Economic
     Advisors, 100
white supremacy, 105–6, 114, 129, 145,
     150
Whitehorn, Laura, 130, 135, 137

Whitman, Walt, 177

Wieseltier, Leon, 116, 118–19

Wild Bunch, The, 194

Wilde, Oscar, 38

Williams, Robert, 147

Willis, Ellen, 119

Wolfowitz, Paul, 9, 35, 53

Woman's Legacy: Essays on Race, Sex and Class in American History, 88

women, 30, 42, 74, 78, 82, 84, 86, 88–90, 92–93, 96, 103, 123, 139, 158–60, 167, 177, 183, 188, 190

Women: The Longest Revolution, 86

women's liberation, 160

women's movement, 86, 92, 160

Women's Studies, 84, 86, 88, 92–93, 190

Women's Studies Department, *see* Department of Feminist Studies

World Trade Center, 23, 35, 127, 129

World Voices Festival, 152

Wright, Jeremiah, 104, 107

Y

Yacub, 109

Yale, 99, 107, 179

Yes, Mao More Than Ever, 114

Z

Zinn, Howard, 114

Zionism, 51, 129